A HANDBOOK FOR RIGHT-WING YOUTH

JULIUS EVOLA

A HANDBOOK FOR
RIGHT-WING
YOUTH

FOREWORD BY GÁBOR VONA

ARKTOS
LONDON 2017

Published in 2017 by Arktos Media Ltd.

www.arktos.com

Originally published as *Jobboldali iatalok kézikönyve* by Kvintesszencia Kiadó in Debrecen, Hungary, 2012.

TRANSLATION	SK
	E Christian Kopff
	Anna Gyulai
EDITOR	John B Morgan
COVER AND LAYOUT	Tor Westman
ISBN	978-1-912079-60-5 (Softcover)
	978-1-912079-59-9 (Hardback)
	978-1-912079-58-2 (Ebook)

CONTENTS

Editor's Note vii

Foreword by Gábor Vona ix

1. A Message to the Youth 1
2. Orientations: Eleven Points 4
3. Outlining the Ideal; The Trial of Air 31
4. The Right and Tradition 35
5. Revolution from Above 45
6. What it Means to Belong to the Right 49
7. The Culture of the Right 54
8. Historiography of the Right 59
9. 'Neue Sachlichkeit':
   The Credo of the New German Generations 64
10. For a 'Youth Charter' 83
11. Biological Youthfulness and Political Youthfulness 90
12. Goliardismo and Youth 95
13. The Youth of Yesterday and the Teddy Boys of Today 99
14. The Youth, the Beats, and Right-Wing Anarchists 103
15. Some Observations on the Student Movement 127
16. Psychoanalysis of the Protest 134
17. Against the Young 141

Bibliographical Notes by Róbert Horváth 148

Index 155

EDITOR'S NOTE

This book is a collection of essays that has no equivalent among the original Italian publications by Julius Evola, having been assembled from essays originally printed in Italian periodicals over the course of Evola's lifetime by the Hungarian traditionalists, as described in the Bibliographical Notes. The Hungarian edition of this book was published by the traditionalist house Kvintesszencia Kiadó (www.tradicio. org) in Debrecen, Hungary in 2012. We extend our sincerest gratitude to Dr Tibor Imre Baranyi and the rest of the staff of Kvintesszencia Kiadó for allowing us to create an English edition of this book, and to Gábor Vona, Chairman of the Jobbik party, for giving us permission to use his Foreword.

All of Evola's essays were translated from the original Italian by SK, with the exception of 'Orientations: Eleven Points', which was translated from the Italian by Professor E Christian Kopff. The Foreword and the Bibliographical Notes were translated from the Hungarian by Anna Gyulai. We extend our particular thanks to Prof Kopff and Ms Gyulai, who did their work as volunteers.

The original dates and places of publication for all of Evola's essays are given in the Bibliographical Notes.

The footnotes to the text were added by me, and are so marked; those footnotes which have no attribution were part of the original Italian texts and were added by Evola himself. Where sources in other languages have been cited, I have attempted to replace them with existing English-language editions. Citations to works for which I could locate no translation are retained in their original language. Website addresses for online sources were verified as accurate and available in January 2017.

The Hungarian edition of this book was edited by Dr Tibor Imre Baranyi and Róbert Horváth.

JOHN B MORGAN IV

Budapest, Hungary, 18 January 2017

FOREWORD

by Gábor Vona[1]

Julius Evola is a well-known figure, and yet also still in a way unknown. A large part of the reading public — thanks either to philistinism or to the influence of a very malicious group — reckons the Italian author to be a sort of 'esoteric fascist'. To show how untenable, superficial, and vile this definition is, we won't even bother to respond to it in this Foreword. Julius Evola was one of the greatest thinkers of the twentieth century, and — besides René Guénon[2] — a decisive personality in the propagation of traditionalism.

The subjects of his writings are so extensive, the quality of his works so profound, that they are unprecedented: his writings on hermeneutics, politics, magic, history, yoga, alchemy, Buddhist asceticism, and sexuality are all of fundamental importance. Unlike other great critics of the modern age, he was not only able to describe a general feeling of

---

1 Gábor Vona (b. 1978) was one of the founding members of the political party, Jobbik, in Hungary in 2003, and has served as its Chairman since 2006. He has also been an elected representative in Hungary's National Assembly since 2010. — Ed.

2 René Guénon (1886–1951) was a French writer who founded what has come to be known as the traditionalist school of religious thought. Traditionalism calls for a rejection of the modern world and its philosophies in favour of a return to the spirituality and ways of living of the past. He outlines his attitude toward modernity in *The Crisis of the Modern World*. — Ed.

crisis — though he accomplished this more deeply than almost anyone else — but to provide guidance, and in this guidance there was no corruptive notion, and he made no compromises. The type of aristocracy he advocated was not only an innate capability, but a conscious, reasoned, and preserving programme for life. His oeuvre and his life: the *rebellion of quality*. This book is an anthology, a handbook for Right-wing youth. But what is the Right and who are the youth, according to Evola? We will try to provide a short answer in this Foreword.

For Evola, Right-wing youth is not what common opinion — especially nowadays, and especially here, in Hungary — thinks it is. But before analysing what it is for him, let's briefly look at what our time thinks about it in general. Just like everything else in the modern era, this concept is determined by the monopoly of Left-wing, liberal opinion. And with such power, which isn't even questioned by the majority, the mental horizon of the latter doesn't even go so far as to ask the most basic questions. Well, who could have doubts when 'they said it on television'? The image of 'Right-wing youth' which is made for and devoured by the idiotic, consumer couch potatoes is the following: protesters with masks on their faces, fighting policemen in a cloud of tear gas; primitive, violent, uncontrolled. I don't think that the average person would question this claim, although in many European countries, this description actually matches the extreme Leftist youth as well. So it's not that simple. Not to mention that those who participate in 'street riots' can be driven by very different values and motives. In most cases they are driven by dissatisfaction and desperation, but protest against a particular political situation or a simple lust for destruction can also be motives. In political discourse, the picture is only a little more detailed: it regards Right-wing youth as nationalists who are authoritarian, intolerant, 'xenophobic', and less sensitive to social problems. This description goes a bit deeper than viewing them merely as street fighters, admitting that they have some sort of coherent set of values, but they quickly add to it that 'most elements of the Right are outdated'.

The potential of the 'Right' to offer its own explanations and influence the war of concepts is a lot slimmer than that of the Leftist monopoly on opinion. This is not only because of the narrower possibilities offered by the existing resources, but also because of the vagueness of its own set of concepts; their incoherence, as well as their infection by Leftism and especially liberalism. The everyday Right — according to its own self-image — loves its nation, its historical heritage, its culture, and its symbols. It is anti-Communist, anti-liberal, and pro-order. Therefore the 'Right wing youth' is the person who believes in these values and regards them as guiding principles. But when the Right follows these principles, unavoidably there's a bad feeling about it, considering that its lot in the world at the present time is weakness and an apparently permanent loss of competitiveness against Left-liberal modernism. This negative feeling is not new; it is centuries old. This feeling of being forced to retreat is responsible for the fact that the Right usually believes that while its aims are good, its tools are weak. And from this desperate conclusion almost automatically comes another, no less desperate conclusion: that it should apply the tools of the Left to bring about its own success. The tragedy of this situation is that the tools of the Left are infectious. This creates a political catastrophe which is extremely common nowadays: the landscape of the so-called Right is in reality becoming more and more filled with Leftist ideas, and allows the Left's borders to approach closer and closer, displaying and mainstreaming the pseudo- or fake Rightism. Of course, this results in total confusion, schizophrenia, and a chaos of ideas. And for those who are disenchanted by the play-fighting of the Left and the pseudo-Right over illusory differences, but still have Right-wing motives and intuitions — for them remains the purely external, pointless opposition to the Left, which has been stripped of its intellectual coherence as well as the basis of its ideology and values: *counter-Leftism*, as coined by the Hungarian philosopher András László.[3] And when it uses these destructive tools in its desperate fights, it actually strengthens those stereotypes which are promoted by the Left-liberal side. So we can speak about Left-wing, pseudo-Right-wing, and counter-Leftist youth too, but Evola's book is of course not meant for them.

The author expects a lot more than tactical bargaining or purely external opposition to the Left from the type to whom he's speaking, but to understand what exactly it is that he expects, we have to define what he calls the Right. First, we have to make it clear that he goes far beyond the shallow and 'up-to-date' political definitions used in political discourse today. According to those, the Right is more or less the conservative idea, which manifested in order to confront Left-wing, revolutionary ideas. But here we immediately face the question of what is it that the Right is protecting, conserving, and guarding against Leftist subversion? The author reveals that the modern 'Right' is merely protecting the status quo of the recent past; namely, that bourgeois world which was already thoroughly pervaded by Leftist, liberal, and egalitarian ideas. For him, this is unacceptable. As he wrote, '[T]here is no negotiating with subversion, and . . . concessions made today mean condemning ourselves to being completely overwhelmed tomorrow. We therefore insist on intransigence of the idea, and a readiness to advance with pure forces, when the right moment arrives.'[4]

Being pervaded by Leftist influences is not the only problem of the Right. It is also that its activity is mostly *reaction*, being dependent upon opposition to the Left. Therefore, the real Right shouldn't be created as a weaker and increasingly infected backlash against the

---

3   András László (b. 1941) is the most important Hungarian traditionalist philosopher of the second generation, having been a student of the first Hungarian traditionalist, Béla Hamvas. His work remains untranslated, although an English translation of his book *Solum Ipsum* is in preparation (a draft is online at www.tradicio.org/english/andraslaszloenglish.htm/). — Ed.

4   From 'Orientations: Eleven Points', p. 12. — Ed.

Left, but rather develop its *own, independent* form of action. It's not 'merely polemical or oppositional'[5] action, but in the end it must have a positive self-definition proceeding from the assumption that the real Right must be able to face the 'trial of air'.[6] It must be capable of actively taking the initiative and establishing itself even when it's not engaged in fighting the Left, when there's no support or frame, when it has to define itself in a vacuum. According to Evola, the present 'Right' is incapable of this because it has no intellectual centre. Where it should exist, there's only emptiness. It's like an army without officers or a traveller without a map. The aim should be pure Rightism, which stands upon the intellectual base of the universal Tradition.[7] And this needs to be seriously absorbed. The real Right should not be engaging in spontaneous and uncontrolled action. Its genuine strategy must be preceded by thorough intellectual maturation.

It's no coincidence that present efforts to elaborate the Right's ideology in an intellectual sense seem to contain a lot of gaps when compared to those of the other side. Because what Julius Evola calls the Right — certainly not our current pseudo-Rightism or counter-Leftism! — used to be the dominant and universal worldview prior to modern times. And it's natural that what used to be considered obvious back then needed no elaboration. It didn't need to be written or spoken about. Subversion began as a subterranean current during the so-called 'Renaissance', and then won a decisive victory in the French Revolution. Thus, politically speaking, Leftism was something that was not self-evident. It had to be explained and it needed to create an

---

5   From 'The Right and Tradition', p. 35. — Ed.

6   The title of one of the essays in this collection. — Ed.

7   The notion of Tradition as understood by Evola holds that there is an underlying metaphysical reality which lies at the heart of all authentic religions and mystical traditions, and which remains the same everywhere, even when there are differences in the exoteric practices and doctrines. Traditionalism is also deeply critical of the modern world. — Ed.

alternative intellectual and ideological system. The Left had to work hard in order to explain and elaborate itself. This drive led it to create powerful and decisive intellectual weapons, and by gradually making use of them, it has been moving inexorably towards victory. This was not the outcome because the Left was more correct, but because the Right had no equivalent tools. As discussed before, its desperation came from its being forced to use the instruments of the Left, thus committing the serious crime of tainting itself.

This is why the Right is both in an easy and a difficult situation at the same time: easy, because it represents the universal and natural human order, and difficult, because it suffers from a serious, centuries-old theoretical, strategic, tactical, and practical lag. So there is a lot of work to be done to clarify traditional Rightism, and this little handbook helps this work along remarkably. It's essential that a youth who identifies as Right-wing establishes a correct relationship with those ideas which have been fetishised by modernism: revolution, democracy, equality, bourgeoisie, scientism — and on the other hand, to find the proper relationship with those other, demonised principles: spirituality, hierarchy, organicism, monarchy. This is not to mention the urgent task regarding the clarification of nationalism and con-servativism — two concepts that have been thought to be self-evident.

Now that we were able to present a little bit about what is and what is not the Right for Julius Evola, we can state: this book has been writ-ten for the youth, but it's *not only for the youth*. Youth, as a condition of age, is only of a secondary importance. The author himself likewise makes a distinction between biological, political, and spiritual youth, where these categories don't necessarily match one's actual age. 'We conceive youth not as a matter of age or a biological fact, but essentially as a spiritual attitude, as a tone and style of life.'[8] What matters is that sort of openness, sensitivity, and potential for assuming the correct

---

8   From 'For a Youth Charter', p. 84. — Ed.

attitude toward life and the political attitude that comes from it which
is inevitably more likely to emerge in those who are still at the age of
soul-searching than among those who have already closed their intellectual doors. But taking into account the time in which the essays in
this book were written, which reflect something that holds even truer
nowadays, we see that the world is on such a downward, darkening
road that the possibilities for the real Right are gradually narrowing.
So it's easy to understand that in this regard, biological age is even less
relevant. To put it positively: we are all 'Right-wing youth', or at least
we should all become such. We should all protect, or if we have lost
it, rediscover our ability to be open to such ideas, because those who
lack this openness and sensitivity, some sort of 'pre-Rightism' which
will enable them to ask the right questions about Evola's work, won't
be able to understand him correctly. For those people, politics will
remain a labyrinth consisting of many shades and mixes of Leftism,
pseudo-Rightism, or counter-Leftism. Evola explains it like this: one
will not come to a correct attitude 'by pandering to demagogy and the
materialism of the masses, but in such a way as to reawaken different
forms of sensibility and interest'.[9] (Here I note in brackets, in complete
agreement with the author, that in my opinion, intellectual openness
and searching — contrary to the common opinion of modern political philosophy — is not at all a Leftist, but rather a Rightist approach,
which we could call pre-Rightism, when we take into account that
the final result one will achieve from making use of a correct style of
openness and the proper intellect can only be an arrival at Right-wing
ideology.)

Evola had no illusions regarding the general state of the youth in
his day. He avoids both being overly pessimistic and overly hopeful.
He's a realist. With cutting sharpness, he sees and points out the nar-
rowness of the possibilities inherent in the typical style of rebellion

---

9   From 'A Message to the Youth', p. 1. — Ed.

and quick temper of youth, stemming from their mostly flat values and self-serving style of action, as well as the unavoidable reconciliation and capitulation of the youth of such a background once they reach philistine adulthood. 'As the years go by, the need for most of them to face the material and economic problems of life will no doubt ensure that this youth, having reached adulthood, will adapt to the professional, productive, and social routines of the contemporary world, thereby essentially passing from one form of nothingness to another.'[10] We would be wrong if, in reading this book, we get the impression that almost nothing has changed since these essays were written. The situation has become worse. And here I don't mean the usual banalities typically spoken by older people, who are always complaining that the younger generations are more and more wretched, because the fact is that there is an increasing confusion manifesting in the older generations as well. Irresponsibility and banality, which usually spring from the nature of youth, are now radiating outward to the whole of society. But what is a peculiarity of age for the youth becomes a toxic influence when it affects the older generations of society. Today we see a kind of sick youth cult, where everybody is fighting a desperate, pathetic, and superficial fight against their own biological clock. In general, this tendency is not as it used to be, when youth would run rampant and yet seek an inner seriousness through which they could find meaning in life, something that 'ages' them — on the contrary, nowadays the older generation, with its purely superficial seriousness, is looking for an inner rampage in order to escape from their own lives and 'to be young again'. This infantile adult of our time is chasing biological youth instead of spiritual youth.

But it's not just losing one's spark by submitting to the usual social routines against which youth should be protected, according to Evola. They should also be warned not to drink from a dirty fountain, out of fear of suffering that fate. He knew that there are many intellectual

---

10 From 'The Youth, the Beats, and Right-Wing Anarchists', pp. 104–105. — Ed.

dangers for those youth who are seeking their path, and the infection is even more damaging in the modern age. Darwinism, materialism, psychoanalysis, and existentialism, against which he especially warns the new generations, are for him merely different manifestations of the same — Leftist — principle that leads to nothing more than degradation and humiliation, depriving them of their humanity. The end result of this is nothing but mediocrity amidst the intellectual desert of consumer society, which Evola contrasts with the higher, heroic, and aristocratic approach to life. Even a modest intellect can see that the basis of the modern world order in an economic sense is the need to manufacture endless consumption. But it also has to be understood that all of this — unfortunately — has its intellectual aspects and effects. The artificial drive for ever greater consumption, in its deeper layers, is not about money and profit, but rather the constant state of excitement that it generates, rendering society vulnerable to suggestions from the Left and the rise of an intellectually constraining path leading towards its desired ends. And when societies, regardless of their existential differences, are burning in a permanent state of social and material desire — and clearly this is the situation in the world today — in such condition, it's not only difficult but almost impossible to pursue higher political and ideological objectives. Looking deeply into things, the real problem is not that you can't read for long on an empty stomach, but rather that the stomach of the modern individual is always empty — even when it's physically full. Who cares about an intellectual centre, human dignity, and heroism among the ruins of this world when happiness is just a matter of success in the stock market?

One of the important lessons which we must take from Evola's works — and the traditionalist authors in general — is that world history is not progressing upwards, but is sinking downwards. To understand this, and to accept and live by it, already presumes very serious intellectual capabilities and bravery, as one must sweep off the proverbial table all the progressive, 'enlightened' narratives of the previous centuries. The concept of progress in history is a very intractable element of modern ideology, the seeds of which were planted in a sense by Judaism and Christianity. The intellectual, environmental, political, social, and economic crisis of the twenty-first century betrays unmistakable signs of decline, and yet the majority of society still lives under the hypnotic influence of the idea of progress. They see these negative symptoms as merely the consequences of a temporary confusion, which triumphant humanity will soon overcome using the best weapons that science, technology, and democracy have to offer in order to get back on the upward path. Reading Evola should help us to overcome this superstition, and in understanding him, we do overcome it. Our historical decline is so dramatic and so obvious that understanding it eliminates many of our previous illusions, and subsequently many of our questions, doubts, and insecurities are immediately resolved, understood, and put to rest.

From this, it follows that total misunderstanding and serious shortsightedness has become the most common approach to politics. This stagnation of politics unavoidably causes people to drift into the muddy waters of intellectual aberration and ideological infection. Those who conduct their political thinking and activities without any real intellectual base and centre will — despite their best efforts — become nothing more than the playthings of powers unknown and imperceptible to them. Their situation is as hopeless as trying to distinguish colours with one's eyes covered. And it provides even more evidence regarding the truth about our modern age that such a completely unworthy political role is not repulsive to the majority of the people who are involved in it. On the contrary, they find the same joy in it that they do in extreme sports. They don't suffer in the intellectual desert, but instead recreate it over and over again, making it go deeper and deeper. Its utter futility is clear to see by anyone who experiences the level of today's political debates, follows the futile and empty sessions of parliament, or looks into the eyes of some politicians. Public life is nothing more than a low-level squabble between those who are inspired by nothing more than economic and social interests, which they hope will grant them the good graces of a society which has been degraded to nothing more than social and economic interests.

In opposition to this, Evolian Rightism is based on metapolitics, and is thus beyond everyday politics. The correctness of its heroic, aristocratic approach is very much proven by the fact that it doesn't simply overcome the obsession with the economy and the type of politics based on it, but also the modern age's orientation toward 'achievement' as the sole indicator of success. 'Another circumstance, namely the fact that the stage we have reached makes it unlikely for the struggle against the presently dominant political and social movements to achieve any appreciable general results, ultimately has little weight: the norm here should be to do what must be done, while being ready to fight — if necessary, even a losing battle.'[11] This political approach transcends the paralysing requirements of success and effectiveness, and instead establishes the values of commitment, loyalty, and honour to be undertaken and expressed in deeds, and does this without any sense of frustration, submissiveness, or lacklustre resignation. The Evolian metapolitical approach stems not from today's feeling of disillusionment and impotence, but rather it is rooted in the commitment and the quality of the dignified man, towering over the merely quantitative approach of the petty proletarian and the comfortable philistine.

---

11   From 'The Youth, the Beats, and Right-Wing Anarchists', p. 123. — Ed.

A MESSAGE TO THE YOUTH

(1950)

The age we find ourselves living in clearly suggest what our primary watchword should be: to rise again, to be inwardly reborn, to create a new order and uprightness within ourselves. Those who harbour illusions about the possibility of a purely political struggle and the power of this or that formula or system, with no new human quality as its exact counterpart, have learned no lessons from the past.

We find ourselves in a world of ruins — we should not forget this. And just how much may still be saved depends only on the existence or lack of men who are still capable of standing among these ruins, not in order to dictate any formulas, but to serve as exemplars; not by pandering to demagogy and the materialism of the masses, but in such a way as to reawaken different forms of sensibility and interest.

Not letting oneself go is what is crucial today. In this society gone astray, one must be capable of *the luxury of having a character.* One ought to be such that, even before being recognised as the champion of a political idea, one will display a certain conduct of life, an inner coherence, and a style consisting of uprightness and intellectual courage in every human relationship. All this, in a straightforward manner, with no exhibitionism, big words, or puritanical attitudes. To the impudent 'why bother?' of others, let us clearly and staunchly reply: '*We* cannot act otherwise — this is our life.' If anything truly positive, like a new order, is ever to be attained, it will not be through the craftiness of democratic agitators and petty politicians, but through the natural prestige and recognition of men — of yesterday and even more so of the new generation — who are capable of as much and can vouch for their ideal.

Uprightness, however, implies adequate knowledge. Young people in particular must become aware of the intoxication which has spread across a whole generation through the many concurrent forms of a false view of life, and which has disintegrated this generation and deprived it of the inner strength to defend itself at the very moment it needed it the most. In one form or another, these poisons continue to operate within contemporary culture, science, sociology, and literature: these breeding grounds of infection must be identified and vanquished. Most prominent among them are Darwinism, Marxism, psychoanalysis, and existentialism. These ideologies convey the same degrading influence, the same attack against true man.

Against Darwinism, let us assert the fundamental dignity of the human person and its unique place. This is not the place of a particular, if more evolved, animal species among many others that has differentiated itself through 'natural selection' while always remaining connected to its beastly and primitive origins; rather, it is such that it is clearly removed from the biological level.

Against Marxism and socialism, let us affirm that the economy and economic interests in all their forms have always exercised — and always will exercise — a subordinate function in normal humanity; that history and every healthy sociopolitical structure are determined by forces of a different sort; and that the fundamental fallacy is to believe that material, environmental factors and conditions of affluence, wealth, or poverty play a decisive role for real human progress.

Against psychoanalysis, let us uphold the ideal of a personality which does not relinquish its role; an aware and autonomous personality which retains its sovereignty over the nocturnal and subterranean part of its soul and the demon of sexuality—a personality that is neither 'repressed' nor psychotically split, but which attains a healthy balance of all its faculties by subordinating them to a higher meaning of life and action.

Finally, at the basis of existentialism, one must only acknowledge the truth of a fragmented human being, who has come to identify existence itself with its lowest and most irrational levels, with its darkest and most senseless expressions, wallowing in a sort of self-sadism. Against all this, let us clearly perceive that 'existence' is not the last resort, that existence actually only reaches fulfilment in those who cast their gaze beyond it, those who are capable of subordinating mere living to something more than living.

Such are the lines of overcoming, which ought not to be intellectual and dialectic, but experienced first-hand, and realised in their direct significance for one's inner life and conduct. It is impossible to rise as long as we remain under the influence of such false and deviant ways of thinking. Once free from the poison, we can attain clarity, uprightness, and real strength. Let us repeat this: inner action must precede all other action. Let this especially be perceived by those youths who retain a spark within themselves, so that they may pick up the torch from those who have not yet fallen. When a front of this sort will emerge, no confusion with what is stirring in the world of public squares and 'democracy' will be possible any longer. If we may hope for a future, it will belong to such men: a path will then be found even for political, national reconstruction. But whatever may happen, we shall hold our positions, as an essential aspect must be the ideal heritage of those men who not so long ago stood their ground and fought, even knowing that the battle was lost. In any event, without sinking to a lower level, without confusing the essential with the accidental, what may be done will be done.

ORIENTATIONS: ELEVEN POINTS

(1950)

POINT 1.

There is no point in indulging in wishful thinking with the illusions of any kind of optimism: today we find ourselves at the end of a cycle. Already for centuries, at first insensibly, then with the momentum of a landslide, multiple processes have destroyed every normal and legitimate human order in the West and falsified every higher conception of living, acting, knowing, and fighting. And the momentum of this fall, its velocity, its giddiness, has been called 'progress'. And we have raised hymns to 'progress' and deluded ourselves that this civilisation — a civilisation of matter and machines — was civilisation *par excellence*, the one for which the entire history of the world was preordained: until the final consequences of this entire process has been such as to cause some people at least to wake up.

It is well known where and under what symbols the forces for a possible resistance tried to organise. On one side, a nation that, since it had been unified, had known nothing but the mediocre climate of liberalism, democracy, and a constitutional monarchy, dared to assume the symbol of Rome as the basis for a new political conception and a new ideal of virility and dignity. Analogous forces awoke in the nation that in the Middle Ages had made the Roman symbol of *imperium*[12] its own in order to reaffirm the principle of authority and the primacy of those values that are rooted in the blood, race, and the deepest powers of a stock. And while in other European nations, groups were already orienting themselves in the same direction, a third force in Asia joined the ranks, the nation of the *samurai*, in which the adoption of the outer forms of modern civilisation had not prejudiced its fidelity to a warrior tradition centred upon the symbol of the solar empire of divine right.

No one claims that there was a very clear discrimination between the essential and the accessory in these currents, that in them the idea was confronted by people of high quality who understood it, or that various influences arising from the very forces that had to be combatted had been overcome. The process of ideological purification would have taken place at a later time, once some immediate and unavoidable political problems had been resolved. But even so it was clear that a marshalling of forces was taking shape, representing an open challenge to 'modern' civilisation: both to those democracies that are the heirs of the French Revolution, and to the other one, which represents the extreme limit of the degradation of Western man: the collectivistic civilisation of the Fourth Estate,[13] the Communist civilisation of the faceless mass-man. Rhythms accelerated, and tensions increased until the opposing forces met in armed combat. What prevailed was the massive power of a coalition that did not draw back from the most hybridised of agreements and the most hypocritical ideological mobilisation in order to crush the world that was raising itself and

---

12 *Imperium* designated the authority of the Roman state to rule over its individual subjects. — Ed.

13 In *Men Among the Ruins* (Rochester, VT: Inner Traditions, 2002), Evola defines the Fourth Estate as being the last stage in the cyclical development of the social elite, beginning with the monarchy; in the final phase of history, he says, 'the fourth and last elite is that of the collectivist and revolutionary leaders of the Fourth Estate' (p. 164). — Ed.

intended to affirm its right. Whether or not our men were equal to the task, whether errors were committed in matters of timing, preparation, or the assessment of risks, let us leave that aside, because it does not prejudice the internal significance of the struggle that was fought. Equally, it does not interest us that today history is taking its revenge on the victors; that the democratic powers, after allying themselves with the forces of red subversion to conduct the war all the way to the senseless extremism of unconditional surrender and total destruction, today see their allies of yesterday turn on them as a danger much more frightening than the one they wanted to exorcise.

The only thing that counts is this: today we find ourselves in the midst of a world in ruins. The problem to pose is, do men on their feet still exist in the midst of these ruins? And what must they do, what can they still do?

POINT 2.

Such a problem, in truth, goes far beyond yesterday's coalitions, because it is clear that both victors and defeated now find themselves on the same level, and the only result of the Second World War has been to reduce Europe to the object of extra-European powers and interests. We have to recognise that the devastation we have around us is primarily of a moral character. We are in a climate of general moral amnesia and of profound disorientation, despite all the accepted ways of speaking in common use in a society of consumers and democracy: the surrender of character and every true dignity, an ideological wasting away, the supremacy of the lowest interests, and living day by day, in general characterise post-war man. Recognising this means also recognising that the first problem, the foundation of every other one, is of an internal character: getting up on your feet, standing up inside, giving oneself a form, and creating in oneself an order and uprightness. People who delude themselves today about the possibility of a purely political struggle and about the power of one or another formula or system, who do not possess a new human quality as a precise opposing vision, have learned none of the lessons of the recent past. Here is a principle that ought to be absolutely clear today more than ever: if a state were to possess a political or social system that, in theory, would count as the most perfect one, but the human substance of which it is comprised were tainted, well then, that state would sooner or later descend to the level of the lowest societies, while a people, a race capable of producing real men, men of just feeling and secure instinct, would reach a high level of civilisation and would stay on its feet before the most calamitous tests even if its political system were faulty and imperfect. We should therefore take a firm stand against that false 'political realism' that thinks only in terms of programmes, partisan political issues, and social and economic recipes. All this belongs to the contingent, not the essential. The measure of what can still be saved rather depends on the existence, or absence, of men who stand before us not to recite talking points, but to be models: not yielding to the demagogy or materialism of the masses, but to revive different forms of sensibilities and interests. Beginning with what can still survive among the ruins, and slowly to construct a new man to be animated by means of a determined spirit and an adequate vision of life, and fortified by means of an iron adherence to given principles — this is the real problem.

POINT 3.

As spirit there exists something that can serve as an outline for the forces of resistance and revival: it is the *legionary spirit*. It is the attitude of one who knows how to choose the hardest life, to fight even when he knows that the battle is substantially lost, and to confirm the words of the ancient saga: 'Loyalty is stronger than fire.' Through him the traditional idea is affirmed. It is the sense of honour and shame — not half-hearted measures drawn from half-hearted morals — that creates a substantial difference, an existential difference between beings, almost as though between one race and another race.

On the other hand, there is the realisation that belongs to those in whom what was an end now appears as only a means. They recognise the illusory character of manifold myths, while leaving intact what they know how to follow *for themselves*, on the frontiers between life and death, beyond the world of the contingent.

These forms of spirit can be the foundation of a new unity. What is essential is to seize them, apply them, and extend them from wartime to peacetime, especially this peace that is only a moment of respite and a poorly controlled disorder — until distinctions and a new grouping are established. This has to happen in rather more essential terms than what might be called a 'party', which can only be a contingent instrument in view of given political struggles; in terms more essential even than a simple 'movement', if by 'movement' we understand only a phenomenon of masses and aggregation, a quantitative phenomenon more than a qualitative one, based more on emotional factors than on severe, clear adherence to an idea. What we are hoping for, rather, is a silent revolution, proceeding in the depths, in which the premises are created, first internally and in individuals, of that Order that will later have to affirm itself externally as well, supplanting suddenly, at the right moment, the forms and forces of a world of subversion. The 'style' that has to achieve prominence is that of one who holds his positions out of loyalty to himself and to an idea, in an intense absorption, in a rejection of every compromise, in a total commitment that must manifest itself not only in the political struggle, but also in every expression of existence: factories, laboratories, universities, the streets, and the very personal life of the affections. We need to reach the point where the type of which we speak, which must be the cellular substance of our group, is completely recognisable, unmistakable, and differentiated. Then we can say, 'He is one who acts like a man of the movement.'

This was the commitment of the forces that dreamed of a new order for Europe, but which was often frustrated and misled in realising it by manifold factors. Today that commitment must be taken up again. And today, the conditions are basically better, because the situation has become clearer. We only need to look around, from the public squares all the way to Parliament, to see that our vocations are being tested, and that we have clearly in front of us the measure of what we should not be. Before a world of mush, whose principles are, 'You have no choice', or else, 'We'll have time for morals after we take care of our stomach and our skin.' (I mean 'skin' in the sense of Curzio Malaparte's novel, *The Skin*!)[14] There is also, 'These are not times in which we can permit ourselves the luxury of having character.' Or last and least, 'I have a family.' When we hear these slogans, we know how to give a clear and firm response: 'As for us, we cannot act in any other way. This is our life, this is our essence.' Whatever positive achievements are accomplished today or tomorrow, it will not be by means of the skills of agitators and political operatives, but by the natural prestige and recognition of men both of yesterday and, even more, of the new generation, who are capable of so much and thus vouch for their idea.

POINT 4.

Therefore there is a new substance that must make its way in a slow advance beyond the boxes, columns, and social positions of the past. We need to have a new figure before our eyes to measure our own force and our own vocation. It is important, or rather basic, to recognise that this figure has nothing to do with classes as economic categories and

---

14   Curzio Malaparte (1898–1957) was an avant-garde Italian writer and journalist. Originally a Fascist supporter, he turned against Fascism after covering the war on the Eastern Front for the Italian newspapers. In his 1949 novel *The Skin*, the book's narrator says, 'Our skin, this confounded skin. You've no idea what a man will do, what deeds of heroism and infamy he can accomplish, to save his skin' (*The Skin* [New York: New York Review of Books, 2013]). — Ed.

with the antagonisms related to them. This figure can present itself in the garb of rich as well as poor, of worker as well as aristocrat, of businessman as well as explorer, technician, theologian, farmer, and even a politician in the strict sense. But this new substance will know an internal differentiation, which will be complete when, again, there will be no doubts about the vocations and functions to follow and command; when a repristinated symbol of unshaken authority will reign at the centre of new hierarchical structures.

This formulation defines a direction that calls itself as much anti-bourgeois as anti-proletarian, a direction completely liberated from democratic contaminations and 'social' whims, because it leads to a world that is clear, virile, articulated, and made of men and men's guides. It has contempt for the bourgeois myth of 'security', and the petty life that is standardised, conformist, domesticated, and 'moral-ised'. Contempt for the anodyne fetter that is part and parcel of every collectivist and mechanical system and all the ideologies that attribute to confused 'social' values the primacy over those heroic and spiritual values with which the true man, the absolute person, ought to be de-fined for us in *every* area. Something essential will have been achieved when we revive the love for a style of active impersonality, through which what counts is the work and not the individual. Through this, we become capable of not seeing ourselves as something important, since what is important is the function, the responsibility, the task accepted, and the end pursued. Where this spirit is achieved, many problems will be simplified, including problems of economic and social order, which would otherwise remain insoluble if confronted from outside, without the counterpart of a change of spiritual factors and without the elimination of ideological infections that from the beginning, already hinder every return to the normal; in fact, even the very perception of what normal means.

POINT 5.

It is important not only for doctrinal orientation, but also in regard to the world of action, that the men of the new group precisely recognise the chain of causes and effects and the essential continuity of the current that has given life to the various political forms that are jousting today in the chaos of the parties. Liberalism, then democracy, then socialism, then radicalism, and finally Communism and Bolshevism, only appeared historically as steps taken by the same evil, as stages in which each one prepares the next in the complex unity of a process of decline. The beginning of this process is the point at which Western man shattered the fetters of tradition, rejected every superior symbol of authority and sovereignty, claimed a vain and illusory liberty for himself as an individual, and became an atom instead of a conscious part in the organic and hierarchical unity of a whole. In the end, the atom was bound to find that the mass of the other atoms, the other individuals, had turned against him, and he was dragged into the plight of the kingdom of quantity, of pure number, of masses that are given over completely to materialism and who have no other god than the sovereign economy. In this process there is no stopping halfway down the road. Without the French Revolution and liberalism, there would not have been constitutionalism and democracy; without democracy there would not have been socialism and demagogic nationalism; without the preparation of socialism there would not have been radicalism and, finally, Communism. The fact that today we see these different forms frequently together or in opposition should not prevent an eye that sees clearly from recognising that they belong together. They are linked, they condition one another in turn, and they express only the different steps of the same current, the same subversion of every normal and legitimate social ordering. The great illusion of our days is that democracy and liberalism are the antithesis of Communism and have the power to stem the tide of the forces of the low, what is called the 'progressive' movement in the jargon of the labour unions. This illusion is like saying that dusk is the antithesis of night, that an illness's incipient stage is the antithesis of its acute and endemic stage, or that a diluted poison is the antithesis of the same poison in its pure and concentrated state. The men in the government of this 'liberated' Italy have learned nothing from the recent past, although its lessons are repeated everywhere monotonously. They continue their pitiful game with political conceptions that are out of date and empty in the parliamentary Mardi Gras, this *danse macabre* on a dormant volcano. What is in our possession is the courage of radicalism, the No spoken to political decadence in all its forms, both of the Left and of the supposed Right. And we must be especially aware of this: that there is no negotiating with subversion, and that concessions made today mean condemning ourselves to being completely overwhelmed tomorrow. We therefore insist on intransigence of the idea, and a readiness to advance with pure forces, when the right moment arrives.

Naturally this also implies ridding ourselves of ideological distortion, which unfortunately is widespread even in some of our young people. It is because of this that they concede some of the excuses for the destructions that have already taken place, deluding themselves with thinking that, after all, they were necessary and will serve the cause of 'progress': that we should be fighting for something 'new', awaiting us in a definite future, instead of for truths that we already possess. This is because, always and everywhere, although these truths appear in different forms, they have been the foundation for every correct type of social and political organisation. Young people need to reject these fads and whims. We should learn to laugh at people who call us 'on the wrong side of history' and 'reactionaries'. There is no such thing as History, this mysterious entity with a capital H. Men make and unmake history, provided they are *really* men. What is called the course of history is more or less the same thing as what is called 'progressivism' in Left-wing circles, and it aims at only one thing today: to foment passivity in the face of the current that is getting stronger and carries us continually lower. As to the charge of 'reactionary', ask them the following question: while you are acting, destroying, and profaning, do you then want us not to 'react', but to stand by passively watching, or maybe even shouting, 'Good work, keep it up!' We are not 'reactionaries' only because the word is not strong enough, and especially because *we* start from what is positive, and we represent what is positive — values that are real and original, and we do not need the light of any 'sun of the future'.

In the face of our radicalism, in particular, the antithesis between red 'East' and democratic 'West' appears irrelevant. An eventual armed conflict between these two blocs appears to us even more tragically irrelevant. If we look only at the immediate future, the choice of the lesser evil is certainly a reality because the military victory of the 'East' would imply the immediate physical destruction of the last representatives of the resistance. But from the point of view of the idea that inspires them, Russia and North America can be considered as two tongs of the same pincers that are tightening definitively around Europe. In them we see the same foreign and hostile force, acting in different but converging forms. The forms of standardisation, conformism, democratic levelling, frantic overproduction, the more or less arrogant and explicit cult of the expert ('brain trust'), and the petty materialism of Americanism can only clear the road for the final phase, which is represented in the same direction by the Communist ideal of the mass man. The distinctive trait of Americanism is that the attack on quality and personality is not accomplished by means of the brutal coercion of a Marxist dictatorship and the care of the state, but takes place almost spontaneously, by means of a civilisation that does not recognise ideals higher than wealth, consumption, profit, and unchecked economic growth — an exaggeration and *reductio ad absurdum* of what Europe herself has chosen. This is what the same motives have created there or are in the process of creating. On both sides we see the same primitivism, mechanical reductionism, and brutality. In a certain sense Americanism is for us more dangerous than Communism, because it is essentially a kind of Trojan horse. When the attack against those values of the European tradition which yet survive are found in the direct and naked form that belongs to the Bolshevik ideology and Stalinism, it still provokes some reactions and certain lines of resistance, even if weak ones, can be maintained. Things are different when the same evil acts in a subtler manner and the transformations take place insensibly on the level of custom and a general worldview, as is the case with Americanism. By thoughtlessly submitting to the influence of Americanism under the flag of democracy, Europe is already predisposed to the ultimate abdication, and this could come about without the need for a military catastrophe, but more or less the same point could be reached in a 'progressive' fashion after a final social crisis. Again, there is no stopping halfway down the slope. Americanism, willy-nilly, is working for its ostensible enemy: collectivism.

POINT 6.

Our commitment to a radical reconstruction is directly relevant here because it insists there can be no dealings not only with every variety of Marxist and socialist ideology, but likewise with what in general can be called the *hallucination,* or the *demonic possession* by the economy. We are dealing here with the idea that in both the individual and collective life, the economic factor is the important, real, and decisive one; that the concentration of every value and interest upon the field of economics and production is not the unprecedented aberration of modern Western man, but on the contrary something normal; not something that is, possibly, an ugly necessity, but rather something that should be desired and exalted. Both capitalism and Marxism are trapped in this closed and dark circle. We need to break this circle wide open. As long as we talk about nothing else but economic classes, work, wages, and production; and as long as we delude ourselves that real human progress and the genuine elevation of the individual is conditioned by a particular system of distribution of wealth and goods, and therefore has to do with poverty and ease, with the state of prosperity *à la* the United States or with that of utopian socialism, we yet remain on the same level as that which we need to combat. We need to assert the following: that everything that relates to economy and the view of economic interest as a mere satisfaction of physical needs has had, has now, and always will have a subordinate role in a normal humanity. Beyond this sphere we need to separate an order of superior values which are political, spiritual, and heroic; an order that — as we already said — does not recognise, or even admit, 'proletarians' or 'capitalists'. It is only in terms of this order that it is proper to define the things for which it is worth living and dying, which establish a true hierarchy, which differentiate new ranks of dignity, and, at the top, place on the throne a superior function of command, an *Imperium*.

In light of this, we need to eradicate many weeds that have taken root here and there, sometimes even in our own field. What, after all, is this chatter regarding a 'state of labour',[15] of 'national socialism', of the 'humanism of work', and similar expressions? What are these more or less openly proclaimed appeals for an involution of politics into the economy, as if in a renewal of those problematic tendencies toward 'integral corporatism', that was basically headless, but which in Fascism fortunately found its way barred? Why do we see the slogan of 'socialisation' considered as a type of universal cure-all and the elevation of the 'social idea' to a symbol of a new civilisation that, who knows how, is supposed to be beyond 'East' and 'West'?

These slogans — we need to acknowledge it — are the dark sides present in quite a few minds that admittedly are in other respects

---

15   The Fascists sometimes referred to their regime as the 'state of labour', implying that it was primarily a workers' state. This became an even greater ideal in the post-Fascist Republic of Italy. — Ed.

found on our side. With this way of talking they think that they are being faithful to a 'revolutionary' commitment, while they are only obeying suggestions stronger than they are. A degraded political environment is full of them. Among these suggestions, the 'social question' re-enters. When will they finally realise the truth? Marxism did not arise because of the existence of a real social question, but the social question arises — in countless cases — only because Marxism exists, in other words artificially, or in terms that are almost always unsolvable, because of agitators, who are notorious for 'raising class consciousness'. Lenin expressed himself very clearly about them, when he refuted the spontaneous character of revolutionary proletarian movements.[16]

It is starting with this premise that we should act, above all, in the direction of ideological *de-proletarianisation*, by disinfecting those parts of the people which are still healthy of the socialist *virus*. Only then can one or another reform be studied and implemented without danger, according to true justice.

Thus, as a particular case, we can examine in what spirit the corporative[17] idea can again be one of the foundations of reconstruction. I mean corporatism not so much as the state's general system of composition, an almost bureaucratic system that maintains the deleterious idea of classes arrayed against one another, but rather as the demand that we must reconstruct within each business that unity and solidarity of differentiated forces which have been prejudiced and shattered, on the one hand, by capitalist prevarication (which has been followed by the

---

16   Lenin devotes the second chapter of his book *What is to be Done?* to a refutation of this notion. — Ed.

17   Present-day readers may be tempted to think of the term 'corporative' and 'corporation' as something relating to companies or business ventures. Evola, however, uses the term, as did the Fascists themselves, to describe a type of society in which its citizens are organised into groups based on the function they perform for the body of the entire society itself, such as agriculture, the military, or administration. — Ed.

parasitic type of the speculator and finance capitalist), and by Marxist agitation on the other. We must bring business into the form of an almost military unity, in which the spirit of responsibility, energy, and competence of the man who directs it will bring about the solidarity and loyalty of the working forces associated around him in a common enterprise. The only true task is, therefore, the *organic reconstruction of business*. To do this there is no need for slogans intended to be fawned upon or for low propagandistic and electoral ends, which represent the spirit of sedition of the lowest strata of the masses, a spirit which is disguised as 'social justice'. In general, we should restore the style of active impersonality, dignity, and solidarity in producing a style that belonged to the ancient corporations of artisans and professionals. We need to outlaw the trade union movement with its 'struggle' and its acts of real blackmail, of which we meet too many examples today. But, let us say again, we need to reach this point by starting from the inside. The important point is that against every form of *ressentiment*[18] and social antagonism everyone should recognise and love his own station, one that fits his own nature, also recognising in this way the limits within which he can develop his own possibilities and achieve his own perfection, because an artisan that acquits himself perfectly in his function is without doubt superior to a king that rejects and does not live up to his dignity.

In particular, we can allow a system of technical competences[19] and corporative representations to replace the partisan parliamentary system, but we should keep in mind that the technical hierarchies, on the whole, can signify only a step in the integral hierarchy. They concern the order of means, to be subordinated to the order of ends, to which alone corresponds the really political and spiritual part of

---

18   *Ressentiment*, literally 'resentment' from French, suggests the endless repetition of the disgust that one feels towards a person or thing, resulting in a deep-seated aversion that becomes part of a person's essential nature. — Ed.

19   'Competences' here refers to specialised areas of professional knowledge. — Ed.

the state. Speaking instead of a 'state of labour' or of production is the same as making a whole of the part, as clinging to what amounts to a human organism reduced to its merely physical and vital functions. Our standard can be neither such an obtuse and dark thing nor the 'social' idea. The true antithesis in front of 'East' as well as 'West' is not the 'social ideal'. It is instead the *integral hierarchical idea*. Confronted with that, no uncertainty is acceptable.

POINT 7.

If the ideal of a virile and organic political unity was already an essential part of the world that was overwhelmed — and through it in Italy the Roman symbol was also recalled — we should also recognise the cases in which such a demand took the wrong path and was nearly aborted in the mistaken direction of '*totalitarianism*'. This, again, is a point that must be seen clearly, so that the two sides are precisely distinguished and, also, so that we do not furnish arms to those who want to confuse matters for reasons we have seen. Hierarchy is not hierarchism. (The latter is an evil that unfortunately tries to spring up in a minor key every once in a while.) The organic conception has nothing to do with a state-worshipping sclerosis and a levelling centralisation. As for individuals, both individualism and collectivism are really overcome only when men stand in front of men, in the natural diversity of their being and their dignity. And as for the unity that ought to, in general, impede every form of dissociation and absolutising of the particular, the unity must be essentially spiritual and of a central orienting influence; an impulse that, depending on the realms, assumes very differentiated forms of expression. This is the true essence of the 'organic' conception, which is opposed to rigid and extrinsic relations appropriate to 'totalitarianism'. In this framework the demand for the dignity and liberty of the human person, which liberalism knows how to conceive only in terms that are individualistic, egalitarian, and privatised, can be realised integrally. It is in this spirit that the structures of a new political and social order must be studied, in solid and clear articulations.

But these kinds of structures need a centre, a highest point of reference. A new symbol of sovereignty and authority is necessary. The commitment, in this regard, must be precise. Ideological tergiversations cannot be permitted. It is important to say clearly that we are dealing here only secondarily with the so-called institutional problem. We are dealing especially with what is necessary for a specific *climate*, for the fluency that ought to animate every relationship of loyalty, dedication, service, and action with no thought of individual glory, so that we have really overcome the grey, mechanical, and devious aspect of the present political and social world. Given the situation today it will end in an impasse, since at the top it is not capable of any kind of asceticism of the pure idea. The clear perception of the right direction is compromised for many, either by some unfortunate antecedents of our national traditions or, and even more so, by the tragic accidents of yesterday. We can also recognise the inconclusiveness of the monarchical solution, since we can see those people who today only know how to defend the remnant of an idea, a symbol that has been gutted and castrated, like the constitutional parliamentary monarchy. But in an equally decisive fashion we ought to proclaim the incompatibility of our idea with the republican idea. To be anti-democratic, on one hand, and to defend the republican idea 'ferociously' (this is unfortunately the terminology of some representatives of a false intransigence) on the other, is an absurdity that is almost palpable. By republic we mean modern republics. The ancient republics were aristocracies — as in Rome — or oligarchies, these latter often possessing the character of tyrannies. Modern republics belong essentially to the world that came into existence through Jacobinism and the anti-traditional and anti-hierarchical subversion of the nineteenth century. This kind of world, which is not ours, must be left behind. In terms of principle, a nation that is already monarchical and then becomes a republic can only be considered a 'downgraded' nation. In Italy we should not play a mistaken game in the name of loyalty to the Fascism of the Salò Republic,[20] because if, for that reason, we feel we ought to follow the false road of republicanism, we would at the same time be disloyal to something larger and better, and throw overboard the central nucleus of the ideology of the Twenty Years of Fascism, which is its doctrine of the state, in the function of authority, power, *imperium*.

This doctrine alone must be maintained, without agreeing to descend to a lower level or play any group's game. The concrete form of the symbol can for the present be left undecided. The essential task is to prepare in silence the suitable spiritual environment so that the symbol of a superior, untouchable authority may be felt and acquire its full significance once again, to which there cannot correspond the stature of any 'president' of a republic who can be voted out of office. Neither will the stature of a tribune or a people's leader be equal to the task, being the holder of a simple, formless individual power that is deprived of every higher chrism[21] and rests instead on the precarious prestige exercised by him over the irrational forces of the masses. It has been given the name 'Bonapartism'[22] and its significance is correctly recognised not as the antithesis of demagogic and 'popular' democracy, but instead as its logical conclusion: one of the dark apparitions

---

20   The Salò Republic, or more formally the Italian Social Republic, was the government of Fascist exiles which was set up in northern Italy, with German military support, following the occupation of the south by the Allies. Once Mussolini was instated as its head of state in September 1943, Mussolini returned to his socialist roots, and said that he had been prevented from realising the genuine Fascist revolution by political contingencies, and pledged to create a new Fascist state that was much more republican and socialist in nature. — Ed.

21   A type of anointing oil used in many branches of Christianity. — Ed.

22   Bonapartism refers to a circumstance where the ideals of a political revolution are co-opted by a dictator who uses it to further his own power aims, as Napoleon did with the French Revolution. — Ed.

of Spengler's 'decline of the West'.[23] This is a new touchstone for our side: a *sensibility* in respect to all this. Carlyle[24] has already talked of the 'Valet-World', who *has* to be governed by the Sham-Hero',[25] not a real Lord.

POINT 8.

We must clarify another point in an analogous order of ideas. We are talking about the position to take in response to nationalism and the general idea of fatherland. This discussion is all the more relevant, because today many, trying to salvage what can be saved, would like to take up a sentimental and, at the same time, naturalistic conception of the nation. This notion is foreign to the highest European political tradition and is difficult to reconcile with the idea of the state that we have already discussed. Even leaving to one side the fact that we see the idea of fatherland invoked by the most divergent parties, even by representatives of red subversion, this conception is already in fact not relevant to the times, because, on one hand, we are witnessing the creation of large, supranational blocs, while, on the other, the necessity of finding a European reference point is increasingly apparent, a unifying one beyond the inevitable particularism inherent in the naturalistic

---

23 This refers to the book *The Decline of the West* (New York: Knopf, 1926/28), in which Spengler theorised that all civilisations go through an inevitable cycle of ages of rise and decline in power, with the present age, which has been dominated by the West, currently entering its declining period. Spengler's thesis bears some similarity to traditional doctrines, but, as Spengler was a Nietzschean, he did not view his theoretical cycle as being the result of a transcendent, metaphysical reality. — Ed.

24 Thomas Carlyle (1795–1881) was a Scottish writer who was extremely influential in the nineteenth century. His book, *On Heroes, Hero-Worship, and The Heroic in History* (1841), portrays human history as being driven by extraordinary individuals. — Ed.

25 Thomas Carlyle, *On Heroes, Hero-Worship, and the Heroic in History* (London: James Fraser, 1841), p. 350. — Ed.

idea of the nation and still more of 'nationalism'. Still, the question of
principle is more essential. The political level *per se* is one of superior
unities when compared to unities defined in naturalistic terms like
those to which the general notions of nation, fatherland, and people
correspond. On this superior level, what unites and what divides is
the idea: an idea borne by a definite elite and tending to achieve concrete form in the state. For this Fascist doctrine — that in this aspect
remained faithful to the best European political tradition — gave first
place to idea and state as compared to nation and people, and understood that nation and people acquire a significance and a form, and
participate in a higher grade of existence, only within the state. It is
precisely in periods of crisis, like the present, that it is necessary to
hold firmly to this doctrine. Our true fatherland must be recognised
in the idea. What counts is not coming from the same land or speaking
the same language, but sharing the same idea. This is the foundation
and the starting point. To the collectivistic unity of the nation — *des
enfants de la patrie*[26]—such as has increasingly dominated ever since
the Jacobin revolution,[27] we oppose something like an Order in every
situation: men loyal to principles, witnesses of a higher authority and
legitimacy that proceed precisely from the idea. As for practical goals,
today we can hope to reach a new national solidarity, but to reach it we
must not descend to compromises. The presupposition, without which
every success would be illusory, is separating and forming a grouping defined by the idea — as political idea and vision of life. There is
no other way, especially today. In the midst of ruins we must renew
the process of originating; one that, in terms of elites and a symbol
of sovereignty and authority, makes a people become one among the
traditional great states, like forms rising out of the formless. Not un-

---

26 French for 'the children of the Fatherland', the phrase occurs in the first line of *La
    Marseillaise*, the national anthem of France since the French Revolution. — Ed.

27 The Jacobin Club, a political group in eighteenth-century France, was one of the
    driving forces of the French Revolution. — Ed.

derstanding this realism of the idea means remaining on a level that is fundamentally sub-political, that of naturalism and sentimentalism, if not of downright chauvinistic rhetoric.

We must be especially attentive where there is a desire to use national traditions to support our idea, because a complete 'national history' of Masonic and anti-traditional inspiration exists that specialises in attributing the Italian national character to the most problematic aspects of our history, beginning with the revolt of the communes with the support of Guelphism.[28] This historical vision emphasises a tendentious 'Italian character', in which we cannot and do not wish to recognise ourselves, and which we happily leave to those Italians who, with the 'Liberation' and the partisan movement,[29] have celebrated a 'second *Risorgimento*'.[30]

Idea, order, elite, state, men of the Order — we should maintain the battle lines in these terms, for as long as possible.

---

28 Guelph is a thirteenth-century term which was originally coined to name the supporters of the Pope, who were in conflict with the Ghibellines, who supported the imperial power of the Hohenstaufen throne against Papal authority. Evola saw this conflict as highlighting the distinction between priestly and royal authority in the state, since he believed the Ghibelline view to be the only valid one from a traditional perspective. He discusses this at length in *Revolt against the Modern World* (Rochester, VT: Inner Traditions, 1995) and *The Mystery of the Grail* (Rochester, VT: Inner Traditions, 1997). The communes were city-states which retained a degree of independence from their rulers in the Holy Roman Empire. In the 1240s, some of the communes sided with the Guelphs against the Emperor. — Ed.

29 The Liberation refers to the end of Fascist rule, and the partisans were those who fought against the Fascists in northern Italy between 1943 and 1945, many of whom were of a Communist orientation. — Ed.

30 The *Risorgimento* ('resurgence') refers to the conquest and unification of the various states on the Italian peninsula by the House of Savoy, the rulers of Piedmont in northern Italy. — Ed.

POINT 9.

Something must be said regarding the problem of culture. Not too much, however. In fact, we do not overvalue culture. What we call 'worldview' is not based on books. It is rather an internal form that can be clearer in a person without a particular culture than in an 'intellectual' or a writer. We should attribute to the evil consequences of a 'free culture' that is within everyone's reach the fact that the individual is left open to influences of every sort, even when he is the sort of person who cannot be actively engaged with them or know how to discriminate and judge correctly.

This is not the right place to discuss this issue except to point out that, as things stand nowadays, there are specific currents against which today's youth ought to defend itself internally. We have talked first of a style of uprightness and self-possession. This style implies a just knowledge, and young people in particular should recognise the poison which has been given to an entire generation by the concordant varieties of a distorted and false vision of life that has affected their inner forces. In one form or another, these poisons continue to act in culture, science, sociology, and literature, like so many hotbeds of infection that must be identified and attacked. Apart from historical materialism and economism, of which we have already spoken, among the most important of these are Darwinism, psychoanalysis, and existentialism.

Against Darwinism we must reclaim the fundamental dignity of the human person by recognising its true place, which is not that of an individual, more or less evolved animal species among so many others, differentiated by 'natural selection' and always linked to bestial and primitivistic origins. Rather it is one which can be elevated virtually beyond the biological level. Even if there is less talk of Darwinism today, its substance remains. The biologistic Darwinian myth, in one variant or another, has the precise value of dogma, defended by the anathemas of 'science', in the materialism of both Marxist and American civilisation. Modern man has gotten used to this degraded conception, tranquilly recognising himself in it and finding it natural. Against psychoanalysis we should oppose the ideal of an ego which does not abdicate, and which intends to remain conscious, autonomous, and sovereign in the face of the nocturnal and subterranean part of his soul and the demonic character of sexuality. This ego does not feel either 'repressed' or psychotically torn apart, but achieves an equilibrium of all his faculties ordered in accordance with a higher significance of living and acting. An obvious convergence can be noted: authority has been stripped from the conscious principle of the person and the subconscious, the irrational, the 'collective unconscious', and similar ideas from psychoanalysis and analogous schools have been given prominence in its place. In the individual, these correspond exactly to what in the modern social and historical world is represented by the crisis, the movement from below, subversion, the revolutionary substitution of the higher by the lower, and the contempt for every principle of authority present in the modern social and historical world. The same tendency is acting on two different levels and the two effects must end up becoming united in turn.

As for existentialism, even if we distinguish what is properly a philosophy — a confused philosophy — that up until yesterday remained relevant only to narrow circles of specialists, it is necessary to recognise in it the spiritual state of a crisis that has become systematised and fawned upon, being the truth of a shattered and contradictory human type which experiences a liberty by which it does not feel elevated as anguish, tragic fate, and absurdity. Such people feel rather condemned without escape and responsibility to this end in the midst of a world stripped of value and meaning. All this, when the best of Nietzsche had already indicated a way to rediscover a sense of existence and to give oneself a law and a value untouchable even in the face of a radical nihilism, under the banner of a *positive* existentialism, according to his own expression: that of a 'noble nature'.

Such are the lines of overcoming, which should not be intellectualistic, but lived and realised in their direct significance for the inner life and its own conduct. Getting back on our feet is not possible as long as we remain in any way under the influence of similar forms of a false and twisted way of thinking. Only when you have freed yourself from dependence on drugs can you attain clarity, uprightness, and force.

POINT 10.

In the zone that stands between culture and custom it will be a good idea to explain the proper attitude more clearly. From Communism was launched the standing order of the anti-bourgeois attitude that has also been picked up by the field of culture in certain 'committed' intellectual environments. This is a point which we need to see very clearly. Just as bourgeois society is something intermediate, so there are two possible ways to overcome the bourgeoisie, to say No to the bourgeois type, bourgeois civilisation, and the bourgeois spirit and its values. One possibility corresponds to the direction that leads on to the lowest point of all this, towards a collectivistic and materialised humanity with its 'realism' in the Marxist style: social and proletarian values against 'bourgeois and capitalist decadence'. The other possibility is the direction that combats the bourgeoisie in order to effectively raise oneself beyond it. The men of the new grouping will be, yes, anti-bourgeois, but by means of the aforementioned superior, heroic, and aristocratic conception of existence. They will be anti-bourgeois because they despise the easy life; anti-bourgeois because they will follow not those who promise material advantages, but those who demand all of themselves; anti-bourgeois, finally, because they are not preoccupied with security but love an essential union between life and risk, on all levels, making their own the inexorable character of the naked idea and the precise action. Yet another aspect by which the new man, the basic cell for the movement of reawakening, will be anti-bourgeois and will differentiate himself from the previous generation, is by his intolerance for every form of rhetoric and false idealism, for all those big words that are written with capital letters; for everything that is only gesture, phrase, effect, and scenery. The essential, on the other hand, is a new realism in measuring oneself exactly by the problems that will face us, and in acting so that what counts is not appearance, but being; not gossiping, but accomplishing, in a silent and exact manner, in harmony with related forces and adhering to the command that comes from above.

Whoever knows how to react against the forces of the Left only in the name of idols, the lifestyle, and the mediocre, conformist morality of the bourgeois world, has already lost the battle beforehand. This is not the case for the man who stands on his feet, having already passed through the purifying fire of outer and inner destruction. Just as this man politically is not the instrument of a bourgeois pseudo-reaction, so, in general, he restores forces and ideals older than and superior to the bourgeois world and the economic era. With these forces and ideals he creates the lines of defence and consolidates the positions from whence, at the right moment, the action of reconstruction will blaze forth.

In regard to this, we also intend to restore a commitment that was not achieved, because we know that there was an anti-bourgeois tendency during the Fascist period that wanted to express itself in a similar direction. Unfortunately, here too the human substance was not equal to the task, and it was possible to make rhetoric even from the steadfast rejection of rhetoric.

POINT 11.

Let us briefly consider a last point: relations with the dominant religion. For us, the secular state, in whatever form, belongs to the past. In particular, we oppose that travesty that has become known in certain

circles as the 'ethical state',[31] the product of a broken-winded, spurious, empty 'Idealist' philosophy that attached itself to Fascism,[32] but
by its nature was able to give equal support, by the simple device of a
'dialectical' game of dice, to Croce's[33] anti-Fascism.

But if we oppose similar ideologies and the secular state, for us
a clerical and clericalising state is equally unacceptable. A religious
factor is necessary as a background for a truly heroic conception of
life, such as must be essential for our group. It is necessary to feel the
evidence in ourselves that beyond this earthly life there is a higher
life, because only someone who feels this way possesses a force that
cannot be broken or overwhelmed. Only this kind of person will be
capable of an absolute leap. When this feeling is lacking, challenging
death and placing no value on his own life is possible only in sporadic
moments of exaltation and in an unleashing of irrational forces; nor is
there a discipline that can justify itself with a higher and autonomous
significance in such an individual. But this spirituality, which ought
to be alive among our people, does not need the obligatory dogmatic
formulations of a given religious confession. The lifestyle that must
be led is not that of Catholic moralism, which aims at little more than
a domestication of the human animal based on virtue. Politically,

---

31　The Fascist state made attempts to instil morality in the Italians, particularly
　　in the area of sexual mores; in *Fascism Viewed from the Right* (London: Arktos
　　Media, 2013), Evola condemns such efforts as belonging to 'little morality' and
　　of being bourgeois in character. — Ed.

32　Evola is referring to Giovanni Gentile (1875–1944), who was Italy's leading
　　philosopher in the Idealist tradition. He was among the most important theore-
　　ticians and intellectual spokesmen of Fascism. His ideas contributed to the idea
　　of the 'ethical state'. Idealism comprises many different schools of thought, but
　　its basic premise is that reality as we perceive it is concocted in our minds, and
　　is a product of thought, rather than something that is objectively real. — Ed.

33　Benedetto Croce (1866–1952) was a highly influential Italian art critic, sena-
　　tor, and a philosopher in the Idealist tradition. He initially supported Italian
　　Fascism, but by 1925 he had become an opponent of the regime. — Ed.

this spirituality can only nourish diffidence before everything that is an integral part of the Christian conception, like humanitarianism, equality, the principle of love, and forgiveness, instead of honour and justice. Certainly, if Catholicism were capable of making a capacity for high asceticism its own, and precisely on that basis to make of the faith the soul of an armed bloc of forces, almost like a resumption of the spirit of the best aspects of the Middle Ages of the Crusades — almost a new order of Templars that will be compact and inexorable against the currents of chaos, surrender, subversion, and the practical materialism of the modern world — in a case like this, and even if at minimum it held firm to the positions of the *Syllabus*,[34] we would choose it without hesitation. But as things stand — given, that is, the mediocre and essentially bourgeois and parochial level to which practically everything that is confessional religion has descended, and given its surrender to modernism and the growing opening of the post-conciliar Church of '*aggiornamento*'[35] to the Left — for our men the mere reference to spirit can suffice, precisely as evidence of a transcendent reality. We must invoke it to inoculate into our force another force, to feel in advance that our struggle is not only a political struggle, and to attract an invisible consecration upon a new world of men and leaders of men.

* * *

These are a few essential guidelines for the battle we have to fight, directed especially to young people, so that they may grasp the torch and the commitment from those who have not fallen, learning from the errors of the past and knowing well how to distinguish and revise everything that was effected by and is still effected today by contingent

---

34 The *Syllabus Errorum*, or *Syllabus of Errors*, was issued by Pope Pius IX in 1864, and was primarily an attack on modernist and liberal social trends. — Ed.

35 Meaning 'bringing up to date', the term was used by those who felt that the Vatican needed to update its ideas in keeping with modern trends, and was a crucial term used during the Second Vatican Council in the 1960s. — Ed.

situations. It is essential not to sink to the level of our adversaries, not to be reduced to manipulating simplistic slogans, and not to insist excessively on the past, which, even if worthy of being remembered, does not have the contemporary and impersonal value of the force-idea.[36] It is likewise mandatory not to yield to suggestions of a false politicising realism, which is the weak point of every 'party'. And, yes, our forces must also act in the hand-to-hand political struggle in order to create room for us to manoeuvre in the present situation and to limit the assault, otherwise unopposed, of the forces of the Left. But beyond that it is important, indeed essential to form an elite that can define an idea with intellectual rigor and intellectual intransigence in rapt intensity. We must unite around this idea and affirm it, especially in the form of the new man, the man of the resistance, the man who stands upright among the ruins. If it is granted to go beyond this period of crisis and unsteady and illusory order, the future will look to this man alone. The destiny that the modern world has created for itself is now overwhelming it. Even if it is not fated to be contained, if we stand by these premises, our inner state will be maintained. Whatever happens, what can be done will be done, and we shall belong to that fatherland that no enemy will be able to occupy or destroy.

---

36 Evola borrowed this concept from Georges Sorel, who used the term 'force-idea' to describe ideas, akin to myths, which could be used to motivate the masses. — Ed.

OUTLINING THE IDEAL: THE TRIAL OF AIR

Dedicated to Youths and Intellectuals

(1952)

Ancient initiation rites would require a neophyte to pass an inner trial, symbolically referred to as the trial of water or even the trial of air. In everyday material life, we are used to solid things which provide something unyielding to hold onto, thus giving us some support even when it is a matter of reacting against them. This is the 'non-I' of which the I usually stands in need in order to perceive itself, almost by way of contrast. The neophyte would be asked to display a capacity for active engagement even in the absence of any support of this kind, even when not having a solid, consistent, and resistant element such as earth around or below him, but a fluid one, such as air or water. The neophyte could therefore prove his freedom, the faculty of performing an act which was truly his own, coming from within.

All this might also be applied to the political domain, in particular with regard to the forces and men of the national front, starting with the MSI.[37] It would be interesting to make such forces and men undergo a 'trial of air'. This is what we mean: let us suppose that the current government should suddenly fall; that the exceptional laws were revoked and many injustices redressed; that Article 16[38] were abolished; and so on — in other words, let us suppose that at a given moment an 'all clear' were issued.

Well, what would happen under such circumstances? Would we witness a capacity analogous to that of the neophytes who pass the 'trial of air'? Or is it rather the case that some would undergo a crisis, while others would remain speechless? This is precisely how things stand: if we leaf through the more nationalist-oriented newspapers, we will find that most of them are almost exclusively filled with polemics, attacks, and criticism. This means that most of the forces are mobilised *in reaction to* the enemy, that they find their *raison d'etre* in the latter and are, so to speak, activated by him. But what if the enemy ceased to be? For many, that would be a sad day. They would no longer know what to say, write, or do. At any rate, what they would say, write, and do would be out of joint with what would be expected of them, based on their previous polemical and aggressive stance.

Here we are not referring so much to the practical side, that is: we are not asking to what extent trained 'cadres' are to be found in our ranks, men of an adequate stature, knowledge, and expertise to

---

37 The Movimento Sociale Italiano, or Italian Social Movement, was formed in 1946 by former members of the Fascist Party in an attempt to carry on the legacy of Fascism. It continued until 1995, when it was replaced by the more moderate nationalist National Alliance, which in turn was merged into Silvio Berlusconi's The People of Freedom party in 2007. — Ed.

38 Article 16 of the peace treaty that was signed between the Allies and Italy in 1947 reads: 'Italy shall not prosecute or molest Italian nationals, including members of the armed forces, solely on the ground that during the period from June 10, 1940, to the coming into force of the present Treaty, they expressed sympathy with or took action in support of the cause of the Allied and Associated Powers.' — Ed.

replace the current political class at the hypothetical moment of the 'all clear' and to establish the true — organic, monolithic — state. Let us take the level of doctrine. As is well known, many people ask themselves: 'Ultimately, what does the MSI *want*? What do the national forces want?' It is difficult to give this question a clear answer in terms of doctrine. The problem of pro- or anti-Atlanticism, that of tactical coalitions or alliances, the relationship with the Church, and so on are only strategic issues and contingent questions; and in any case, a clear solution to them could only be found starting from a well-defined doctrine concerning the values and principles of political organisation.

Only very few among the writers and 'intellectuals' of the MSI take an interest in these topics and go beyond generic formulas, catchwords, and vague patriotic references. In fact, the situation is such that it would be better for them not to do anything of the sort, because if one were to really follow them and believe that what one is fighting for is their political ideal, the consequences which would be drawn from it would be rather grievous: for the few ideological insights that have been adequately defined betray socialist[39] tendencies that are more than dubious and, in our view, represent a genuine betrayal of the main party line, which is rather in keeping with the highest European political tradition.

Those few intellectuals or journalists with the wrong vocation aside, what we find is almost a vacuum in what ought to be a central area: the area of pure political doctrine, with reference — let me stress this once again — to *positive* formulations, as opposed to polemical or contingent ones. Is it fear? Is it aversion towards any form of intellectual discipline? But this is like fighting aimlessly, in hand-to-hand combat, with no General Staff, with no army in which individual actions are coordinated and acquire meaning in the light of well-defined

---

39 Evola specifically uses the word *socialistoidi* here, which has a disparaging connotation, unlike the usual word for socialism, *socialiste*. — Ed.

objectives. The predominant situation is this: pro-MSI publications increasingly tend to feature articles that set out from the subject of the day to launch attacks and polemics, rather than articles which focus on ideas and contribute to defining some principles, a style, and a view of life and the state.

This is an issue on which those harbouring 'revolutionary' ideals should also reflect. It is worth bearing in mind that the main revolutions in Europe were preceded by a precise doctrinal preparation. Such was the case both with the French Revolution and the Communist and National Socialist ones. It was far less the case with Fascism, where activism largely preceded doctrine — hence the weaknesses and ambiguities of the Fascist system. Lending form to the ideal, lending form to some 'cadres': this is the essential task. And in our cases the existing circumstances might even be conducive to this goal. If Scelba's repressive measures[40] were really to be applied, one might take advantage of this to limit every exterior, polemical, or simply aggressive expression as far as possible, so as to focus instead on the inner dimension and thus carry out serious preparative work. It was in exile and silence that Lenin formulated — systematically and lucidly — the doctrine destined to overthrow old Russia. It was in prison that Hitler laid down the ideological positions for his struggle. All this springs not from mere activism, from reacting and striking here or there, but from the building up of an intensity which retains the seed of an impetus for a more renovating force.

---

40 Mario Scelba (1901–1991), born in Sicily, was a Christian Democrat who was Minister of the Interior, with some interruptions, from 1947 until 1955, and was then Prime Minister of Italy in 1954–55. He became known as the 'Iron Sicilian' for his harsh repressive measures as Minister against both Communists and neo-Fascists. He also wrote the Scelba law which formally banned Fascism, and his anti-Fascist laws remain in force to this day. He also helped to set up NATO's clandestine Gladio network in Italy. — Ed.

THE RIGHT AND TRADITION

(1972)

The idea of the Right is eliciting interest across a rather wide and varied range of milieus nowadays. Given the political and cultural turmoil of contemporary Italy, this is certainly a positive sign. However, when an idea finds greater resonance, it almost invariably loses its clear definition, and endures more as a formula than in terms of any specific content. This also applies to the idea of the Right, particularly when it is not merely applied to its original level, which is to say the political level, but is considered a general attitude.

In this context, one issue which may prove of particular interest is that of the relationship between the concept of the Right and that of Tradition.[41] It is necessary to focus on this issue, if one wishes to assign a positive content to the concept of the Right, as opposed to a merely polemical or oppositional one.

---

41 Evola here uses the term Tradition in the same sense as René Guénon; namely, as a set of transcendental metaphysical principles which lies at the heart of all authentic religions, and which remains the same even when there are differences in the exoteric practices and doctrines. Evola fully explicated his doctrine of Tradition in his 1934 book, *Revolt against the Modern World.* — Ed.

The merely polemical content of the Right has been implicit ever since its origins, for it is a well-known fact that the Right was called as such because of the physical place in Parliament[42] which was occupied by those representatives which sided against the revolutionary MPs, who thereby came to be defined as the 'Left'. In the assemblies of the old regimes, however, the opposition was not between individuals on the same footing. These were for the most part monarchical regimes, and the Right acted not for any cause of its own, but rather in defence of the higher principles of authority and order eminently enshrined at the very head of the state. Besides, even the so-called 'opposition' originally had a functional character, since idealism and a cooperation — an idea distinctly expressed by the English formula 'His Majesty's most loyal opposition'[43] — were expected of its representatives. Only with the rise of revolutionary ideologies and movements did the definition of the Right and the Left as fully opposed factions emerge. Within this framework, the Right naturally acquired a conservative tendency.

The process just described points to some essential concepts related to the overall issue we here wish to consider. With the decline of the 'ancient regime', what also partly disappeared, or became more feeble, was a *positive* higher principle of reference. Already on the political level, it is easier to say what the Right does not want and fights than what it wants and wishes to defend — for here divergences of no little import in terms of content may emerge.

Even when, by extension, one speaks of a Right-wing cultural orientation and worldview, a purely negative definition is easier to give, yet it is clearly incomplete. It is necessary to introduce positive principles, in order to underpin a genuine antithesis: principles

---

42 Evola is referring to the National Assembly which emerged following the French Revolution in 1789. — Ed.

43 This phrase first came into use in the English Parliament in 1826. — Ed.

which ultimately are bound to have a 'traditional' character. Only, it is opportune to note that one must then draw upon a particular and eminent concept of tradition which, with the definition given by a corresponding current of thought, has commonly come to be spelled with a capital letter — and not merely for rhetorical emphasis.

A generic traditionalism of the empirical or simply historical sort is not enough. But often this is all the factions of the political Right amount to. We have already noted that it is quite natural for it to be 'conservative'; as such, it is also 'traditional', in the sense that it refers to a given system of principles and institutions which it seeks to maintain or safeguard. At this level, the Right clearly remains within the boundaries of factuality, or indeed relativity, the point of reference merely being the one which it has happened to inherit and which is only assigned any value, as something to be conserved and preserved, for this reason.

However, a broader and loftier conception may be found by taking enduring values of a universal sort as a reference. *It is these values which may lend a positive content to a true Right.* In this sense, the concept of Tradition applies to a system in which 'all activities are in principle ordered from above and have an upward direction'.

Consequently, the natural and fundamental prerequisite for a 'traditional' Right would appear to be the acknowledgement of a reality of a higher order which also possesses a deontological, which is to say normative, character. In ancient times, people would speak of an overworld opposed to the world of becoming and contingency. Later, religion came to serve as a basis. In the latter case, however, limiting conditionings may emerge if there is an institutionalised positive religion, a Church — the concrete risk being that it comes to monopolise spiritual authority (historically, this trend is what triggered the Ghibelline[44] 'protest'). So it is preferable to keep to a more neutral level, to assert strictly religious points of reference only in a subordinate way, and to rather draw upon the concept of 'transcendence'. This means transcendence compared to everything simply human, physical, naturalistic, and materialistic, which is not to say detached or abstract. Indeed, one might, somewhat paradoxically, speak of 'immanent transcendence': for it is also necessary to refer to a genuine formative, energising, and organising power which operates precisely 'from above' and in an upward direction. This may be regarded as the ultimate point of reference for the traditional orientation, regardless of the particular, concrete forms in which it may manifest itself.

Consequently, the background of any Right possessing a 'traditional' content, and of any corresponding worldview and outlook on life, should be of an analogous sort: it should be a spiritual background. In any case, it is only by keeping to this level that one may lend a superior foundation and legitimation to each particular stance of the traditional Right. This is bound to be hierarchical and aristocratic; bound to posit clearly differentiated hierarchies of values and assert the principle of authority; bound to oppose the world of quantity, the masses, democracy, and the rule of the economy; bound to emphasise what is truly worthy of effort and to completely subordinate its own particular interests to the attainment of anagogical virtue, that virtue which draws upwards ('upwards' as the counterpart to 'from above') — precisely by being anchored 'above', to that reality of a higher order. It has quite rightly been observed that personality, in the eminent sense of the

---

44 Ghibelline is a thirteenth-century term which was originally coined to name the supporters of the imperial power of the Hohenstaufen throne against Papal authority. They were in conflict with the Guelphs, who favoured the rule of the Pope. Evola saw this conflict as highlighting the distinction between priestly and royal authority in the state, since he believed the Ghibelline view to be the only valid one from a traditional perspective. He discusses this at length in *Revolt against the Modern World* and *The Mystery of the Grail*. — Ed.

term, only exists when it is open to the supra-personal, and this corresponds precisely to the spirit and climate of Tradition.

No doubt, for the establishment of a Right of such kind, one not confined to political and social stances — since these should only come to be defined and applied as a consequence — what would be required is a major effort of demolition, along with a vocation and qualifications which are difficult to come by nowadays. Courage, too, is necessary — in some cases, more than just intellectual courage. In this respect, a paradoxical convergence might possibly occur between traditionality and revolution. Besides, 'conservative revolution' is not a new term: the expression was already used to designate an interesting cultural-political current in pre-Nazi Germany,[45] where conservation referred not to anything factual but to basic ideas of perennial relevance (Moeller van den Bruck).[46] With respect to modern civilisation

---

45 The Conservative Revolution is a term first coined by Hugo von Hoffmansthal, which has come to designate a loose confederation of anti-liberal German thinkers who wrote during the Weimar Republic. There was a great diversity of views within the ranks of the Conservative Revolutionaries, but in general they opposed both democratic capitalism and Communism in favour of a synthesis of the German (and especially Prussian) aristocratic traditions with socialism. Spengler advocated one form of this doctrine which he termed 'Prussian socialism'. The Conservative Revolutionaries opposed liberalism in all its forms, rejected a return to the Kaiser's Reich, and saw Germany as being culturally tilted more towards Russia than towards France or Britain. The standard scholarly study of the Conservative Revolution is Armin Mohler's *Die Konservative Revolution in Deutschland, 1918-1933* (Stuttgart: F. Vorwerk, 1950), followed by many later revisions and re-printings. — Ed.

46 Arthur Moeller van den Bruck (1876-1925) was one of the principal authors of the German Conservative Revolution. He is best known for his 1923 book, *Das Dritte Reich*, translated as *Germany's Third Empire* (London: Arktos Media, 2012). A follower of Nietzsche, he advocated the idea of a third German empire to replace the Weimar Republic which would embody a synthesis between socialism and nationalism and provide for the needs of all citizens, but within a hierarchical framework based on traditional values. Despite Hitler's appropriation of his book's title, he rejected National Socialism for its anti-intellectual nature in a note he left just prior to his suicide. — Ed.

and society, it may indeed be said that nothing possesses a more revolutionary character than Tradition, which — in proper and Hegelian terms[47] — constitutes the 'negation of a negation': for the latter is what, through 'progress', has desecrated everything and subverted every normal order, leading us to the state we find ourselves in today. This negation must be denied. Thus, a further watchword might apply to the traditional Right: 'revolution from above' — the opposite of all the anarchical tendencies of today, which only amount to a vain and senseless commotion, with no positive counterpart. Its champions are actually incapable of conceiving anything of the sort, even when they do not — either consciously or unconsciously — fall within the orbit of Left-wing ideologies or are not manipulated by the Left.

* * *

Turning our gaze to what is — or has been — labelled Right-wing, some clarifications are in order in the light of what has been argued so far. Talk has been made of the Right as an economic front more or less associated with capitalism, an easy target for Marxism and other forces of subversion. In this respect, a lamentable downgrading is to be observed, although one must acknowledge that even in this material

---

47 From G. W. F. Hegel's *Philosophy of Right* (Mineola, NY: Dover Publications, 2005), p. 35: 'An injury done to right as right is a positive external fact; yet it is a nullity. This nullity is exposed in the actual negation of the injury and in the realization of right. Right necessarily brings itself to pass by cancelling the injury and assuming its place. Addition. — By crime something is altered, and exists as so altered. But this existence is the opposite of itself, and so far null. Nullity consists in the usurpation of the place of right. But right, as absolute, is precisely what refuses to be set aside. Hence it is the manifestation of the crime which is intrinsically null, and this nullity is the essential result of all crime. But what is null must manifest itself as such, and make itself known as that which violates itself. The criminal act is not the primary and positive, to which punishment comes as the negative. It is the negative, and punishment is only the negation of a negation. Actual right destroys and replaces injury, thus showing its validity and verifying itself as a necessary factor in reality.'

sphere there are some structures worth preserving and safeguarding. More generally, there is a Right which is chiefly defined by the conservative tendencies of the bourgeois middle class, and this has especially been the case in Italy. In other countries, the points of references partly stem from the higher level just described. The traditional French Right has essentially been a Catholic and monarchist one, although reservations have been expressed with regard to a certain kind of Catholicism, of the sort embraced by Charles Maurras,[48] when this religion has been taken up as more than just a political background for the Right.

A sort of monarchist mystique is implicit in the Right of the Anglo-Saxon countries, which also have no need to refer to Catholicism alone: Protestantism has served as a point of reference in much the same way. The Protestant Bismarck was a leading exponent of the true Right no less than the Catholic Metternich, or indeed the Catholics de Maistre[49] and Donoso Cortés.[50] With regard to Prussianism, however, one must note a degree of secular involution, in the sense that the reference to anything transcendent is concealed: what stands in the foreground here is a sort of independent ethics, a traditional, innate character training which appears to have a power of its own but ultimately — in its emphasis on the supra-personal — could hardly be justified if it were not a by-product, so to speak, of a previous orientation with a spiritual background (it is worth recalling that Prussianism, and its ethics, first emerged through the secularisation of the Order of the Teutonic Knights).

---

48 Charles Maurras (1868–1952) was a French nationalist counter-revolutionary ideologue who was the founder of the Right-wing Action Française. — Ed.

49 Joseph de Maistre (1753–1821) was a French Counter-Enlightenment philosopher who fled the Revolution and lived the remainder of his life in Italy. He always remained a staunch opponent of democracy and supported monarchical rule. — Ed.

50 Juan Donoso Cortès (1809–1853) was a Spanish Catholic political thinker who opposed the ideals of the French Revolution. — Ed.

Sometimes, people also speak of the Right in relation to political systems of the 'fascist' sort. In this case, however, certain reservations are in order. In a series of essays on the European Right,[51] the authors quite rightly observe that these systems cannot be described as Right-wing in the old, traditional sense of the term, since they are rather marked by the mingling of Right and Left: on the one hand they upheld the principle of authority, but on the other relied on mass parties and embraced 'social' and revolutionary principles of the Left, against which men of the real Right would certainly have taken a stand. More generally, it is misleading to describe a dictatorship as Right-wing, since a dictatorship intrinsically has no tradition of its own, but represents an amorphous constellation of power expressed through a given individuality (what we have in mind here is dictatorship as a type of constitution, not as something transient, imposed by crisis or emergency situations). Machiavelli's Prince does not embody the Right at all; rather, he represents an inversion of relations: while the Machiavellian leader may invoke spiritual or religious values, he will do so by simply endorsing them as a useful means to his rule, without acknowledging their instrinsic worth. The argument could be extended to those principles — including principles of a higher order — which are used simply as 'myths' within the framework of totalitarian dictatorships, which is to say through formulations that enable them to stir or channel the irrational forces of the masses. On the other hand, there is no need to stress the incompatibility of the Right with democracy.

All these considerations confirm the importance of the aforementioned link between the true Right and Tradition.

* * *

51 Hans Rogger & Eugen Weber (eds.), *The European Right: A Historical Profile* (Berkeley: University of California Press, 1966).

In the light of what has been argued, in order to conceive of a 'culture of the Right', it is necessary to acknowledge the emphasising of the values of Tradition as one of its chief duties, and at the same time to avoid any merely 'traditionalistic', which is to say conformist, orientation. The field of Right-wing culture is potentially vast. The historiography and morphology of civilisations ought to play an important part here, since after rejecting all forms of historiography with liberal, Marxist, or progressive leanings, it would be a matter of systematically highlighting everything that embodied traditional principles in previous periods, in such a way as to bring out their paradigmatic character. In this respect, useful contributions have already been provided most especially by the current inspired by René Guénon, a true master of our times. Within the limits of our abilities, we too have put ourselves to a similar task, since in the first part of our work *Revolt against the Modern World*, based on comparative research, we outlined a sort of 'doctrine of the categories' of the 'World of Tradition'.

Once it has established some firm axiological points of reference, a culture of the Right should set itself the task of studying their possible applications with respect to the present state of affairs. The danger of sclerotic conservatism should be overcome by adopting the principle of *homology*. What homology means is not identity but correspondence, not the exact reproduction of formal principles but their reaffirmation and transposition from one level to another, from one set of situations to another. To use a simile, we might compare this to an eddy vanishing from a given point in a current, only to emerge — in accordance with the same law — at a different point: the same yet different, since it is within something which flows — like time or history — that these eddies emerge.

The general methodological guidelines which have been provided may be more concretely defined by considering the different fields with which a culture of the Right should engage, in such a way as to establish a range of practical strategies. The important thing here is to keep to the same course, without yielding to the temptation to adopt accommodating stances, of the sort which may ensure a broader, but less select, field of influence: we must bear in mind that we are working not just for today but also, and especially, for tomorrow — and that, as Hegel puts it, 'The Idea does not hurry'.

* * *

These are far from superfluous considerations, since the apparent popularity of the idea of the Right today — as we noted at the beginning — has often led it to be associated with very different or even spurious attitudes, or at any rate ones hardly reflecting a rigorous and coherent line of thought. But such a line of thought is precisely what is required when it is not a matter of improvising, or merely of endorsing certain political views, but also of defining a more general existential and cultural orientation.

REVOLUTION FROM ABOVE

(1973)

One of the general features of the end times is the exercising of an urge, drive, and action towards radical change from below, and for the sake of what is below, upon existing social and cultural structures. This corresponds to the specific and legitimate meaning of the term 'subversion'.

The premise of this situation is clearly the crisis of the structures in question — be they sociopolitical, or cultural and intellectual ones. Thus the action in question is associated with a questioning of the modern world, bourgeois society, and capitalism, of an order that is reduced to an outwardly contained disorder, and of forms of existence that have lost all higher significance and become dehumanising and a cause of 'alienation' (to use a rather tired term).

The revolt against all these features of a society presenting so many problematic aspects may seem legitimate. But what distinguishes the final times is the lack of any rectifying, liberating, or restoring action from above: the fact that the often necessary initiative and action towards radical change is allowed to be carried out from below — from below, that is, in terms both of lower social strata and lower values. The almost inevitable consequence of this is the shifting of the centre of gravity to a level that is even further down than that of the structures which have entered into crisis and lost their vital content.

In the sociopolitical field, the phenomenon takes such precise forms that it is almost superfluous to focus on them. No one can be so short-sighted as to fail to understand by now what the famous expression 'social justice' really means.

It is not at all real justice — the distributive justice of *suum cuique*,[52] based on a principle of inequality, as already defended by writers beginning with Aristotle and Cicero. Rather, it is a partisan pseudo-justice, exclusively serving the interests of the lowest strata, the so-called 'working class', to the detriment of other classes, in the name of myths whose only purpose is to gradually pave the way for the rise to power of Leftist forces.

This extremely organised, systematic, and almost unrestrainable action from below is often associated with the Rousseauesque lie that the natural, healthy, generous man is only to be found among the lower classes, and hence that the ultimate aim of the subversive movement is a new and effective 'humanism'. There is almost no one capable of countering this action with a vigorous reaction. Besides, the principle of reaction ought to consist of this: the possibility to denounce the fallacies, defects, and degeneration of a system — for instance, the possibility of taking a hard stance against the bourgeoisie and a certain kind of capitalism — starting from a level that is situated above rather than below it, in the name not of petty socialist or proletarian values, but of qualitative, aristocratic, and spiritual ones. Such values should inspire a rectifying action of an even more radical sort, provided truly worthy men and groups are to be found with enough authority and power to prevent or quash any ambition or attempt to carry out a revolution from below. 'Revolution from above' is actually a formula which was already used and partially applied by Bismarck ('the only revolution we know is the revolution from above').[53]

---

52   Latin: 'to each his own', a concept first popularised by Cicero. — Ed.

53   Bismarck and the Prussian aristocracy instituted socialist reforms in Germany, rather than such reforms taking place as a direct result of political action taken by the lower classes. — Ed.

Regrettably, it is becoming increasingly clear that any such prospect is quite foreign to the intellectual horizon of our contemporaries. It is further to be observed that even those who claim to be fighting against the 'established disorder' of the modern world on the basis of correct (yet almost obvious and self-evident) accusations against present-day society and the so-called 'system', even by putting forward values, such as personality and Christianity, do not conceal their sympathy towards what lies below, towards claims raised from below, and towards the pseudo-humanism of the Left, while showing just as much intolerance or lack of understanding for any possible solution within the framework of an order resting on a principle of higher authority, sovereignty, and true justice. As typical examples of this, one might refer to the views held by people such as Mounier[54] and Maritain,[55] or even those of a traditionalist such as Leopold Ziegler.[56]

It is interesting to note the exact inner correspondence between this outlook and other ones in strictly cultural domains. Is it not the case that so-called 'neo-realism'[57] and other, similar tendencies

----

54 Emmanuel Mounier (1905–1950) was a French philosopher who was the primary thinker of the personalist school of thought. Personalism was anti-liberal and therefore viewed as being of the Right, although the personalists were also sympathetic to socialist ideas and valued the individual. — Ed.

55 Jacques Maritain (1882–1973) was a French Catholic philosopher. A political liberal, he defended natural law ethics and developed a system of philosophy called Integral Humanism in order to attempt to reconcile Christianity with liberalism. He also participated in the drafting of the UN's Universal Declaration of Human Rights. — Ed.

56 Leopold Ziegler (1881–1958) was a German philosopher of religion who was influenced by Guénon, and who in turn was influential on the thinkers of the Conservative Revolution, in particular Ernst Jünger and his brother Friedrich Georg, whom he knew personally. — Ed.

57 Neo-realism was a movement in Italian film which began after the fall of Mussolini and lasted into the early 1950s, which sought to portray the plight of the poor and working classes in the aftermath of the war, usually depicted using non-professional actors and with a minimum of artistic stylisation. — Ed.

unjustifiably present only the lowest, most squalid, questionable, and often even obscene and vulgar aspects of life as 'real'? It is as though everything else had nothing to do with what is authentic, sincere, and 'real'.

An even more significant case, which reveals the vast field of action of this tendency, is constituted by psychoanalysis and modern irrationalism. The starting point has been the (in itself legitimate) criticism of blind devotion to 'reason' and abstract intelligence, of the superstructures of the conscious Ego. But this has then led to a downward rather than upward opening of man. Against 'rationalism', mere irrationality and 'life' have been upheld; against the conscious, the unconscious, which has come to be regarded as the only real driving force of the psyche. Here too, then, the result has been a regression, a downward shift of man's centre of gravity. The cause is much the same as that which has been described in relation to the sociopolitical field: the assumption that beyond the 'rational' and its possible abuses one only finds the sub-rational (the unconscious, vital, instinctual, etc.) — and not the super-rational as well, as witnessed by anything that has ever been associated with true human greatness in the history of civilisation.

Similar considerations might be made, so as to provide further parallels, with regard to other contemporary cultural phenomena, such as existentialism and many forms of so-called neo-Spiritualism. We cannot dwell on this in the present essay.[58] It must suffice to have briefly illustrated the underlying tendency common to a whole range of phenomena and what their presence — a marker of the true face of our age — regrettably indicates, namely: the almost complete absence today of anyone capable of standing his ground and acting not from below but from above, in all domains.

---

58 Evola takes up these subjects in *Ride the Tiger* (Rochester, VT: Inner Traditions, 2003). — Ed.

WHAT IT MEANS TO BELONG TO THE RIGHT

(1973)

Right and Left are designations which refer to an already crisis-ridden political society. They did not exist in traditional regimes, at any rate not according to the meaning currently assigned to them. In such regimes an opposition could be found, yet it was never a revolutionary one that challenged the system; rather, it was a loyalist and, in a way, functional opposition: this was the case in England, for instance, where one would speak of 'His Majesty's most loyal opposition'. Things changed with the emergence of subversive movements in recent times: as is widely known, Right and Left originally referred to the place occupied by the opposite parties in parliament.

The term Right acquires different meanings according to one's plane of reference. There is an economic Right, based on capitalism, which does not lack some degree of legitimacy provided it does not abuse its position. Its antitheses are socialism and Marxism.

As for the political Right, strictly speaking it acquires its full meaning only in relation to a monarchy within an organic State: this has especially been the case in Central Europe, and partly in conservative England.

49

Yet it is also possible to leave all institutional assumptions aside and speak of the Right as a spiritual orientation and worldview. Aside from opposing democracy and all 'socialist' myths, belonging to the Right means upholding the values of Tradition as spiritual, aristocratic, and warrior values (possibly with reference to a strict military tradition, as in the case of Prussianism, for instance). Moreover, it means harbouring a certain contempt for intellectualism and for the bourgeois fetishism of the 'cultured man' (the scion of an ancient Piedmontese[59] family paradoxically claimed, 'I divide the world into two classes: the nobility and those with a degree', while Ernst Jünger,[60] for his part, praised a 'healthy illiteracy' as an antidote).

Belonging to the Right also means being conservative, yet not in a static sense. The obvious assumption is that there remains something worth conserving, which raises a difficult problem in relation to the recent past of Italy after its unification: nineteenth-century Italy has

59 Piedmont is a region of northern Italy which initiated Italy's unification following its independence from the Austrian Empire. The House of Savoy, or the governing monarchy of Piedmont, became the monarchs of the Kingdom of Italy. — Ed.

60 Ernst Jünger (1895–1998) was one of the most prominent of the German Conservative Revolutionaries, but that was only one phase in a long and varied career. He volunteered for and fought in the German Army throughout the First World War, and was awarded the highest decoration, the Pour le Mérite, for his service. After the war, he wrote many books and novels, was active in German politics, experimented with psychedelic drugs, and travelled the world. He remained ambivalent about National Socialism at first, but never joined the Party, and he had turned against the Nazis by the late 1930s. He rejoined the Wehrmacht at the outbreak of war, however, and remained in Paris as a Captain, where he spent more time with Picasso and Cocteau than enforcing the occupation. His objections to the Nazis were influential upon the members of the Stauffenberg plot to assassinate Hitler in July 1944, which led to his dismissal from the Wehrmacht. After the war, Jünger's political views gradually moved toward a sort of aristocratic anarchism, and he continued to be a highly celebrated literary figure. — Ed.

hardly left us any legacy of higher values that are worth safeguarding and which might serve as a foundation. Going even further back in time, Right-wing positions are only sporadically to be found in Italian history: what is missing is a moulding unitary force of the sort occurring in other countries, which have acquired solidity through the ancient monarchist traditions of an oligarchy.

Be that as it may, what the claim that the Right must not be characterised by static conservatism means is that certain values and underlying ideas must indeed be there as a firm foundation, but must be expressed in different ways, in keeping with the times so as not to let oneself be overtaken by them. This enables one to avoid being left behind and to grasp, govern, and absorb anything that may emerge as the context changes. It is only in this sense that a man of the Right may conceive of 'progress' — and not as a mere forward movement, as is all too often held to be the case, especially on the Left; in this context, Bernanos[61] quite rightly speaks of an 'escape forward' (*'où fuyez-vous en avant, imbécils?'*).[62] 'Progressivism' is a whim alien to any Right-wing stance. This is also the case because, with respect to the course of history in general and in particular to spiritual values — as opposed to material values, technological achievements, and so on — the man of the Right tends to detect a fall, not any progress or genuine ascent. The developments taking place in present-day society are bound to confirm this belief.

A Right-wing stance is necessarily anti-collectivist, anti-plebeian, and aristocratic: its positive counterpart is thus to be found in the affir-

---

61   Georges Bernanos (1888–1948) was a French author who was a Catholic and a monarchist, and for a time was a member of the Action Française. In spite of his dislike of democracy, he disliked fascism and became an expatriate in Brazil in 1938, becoming a staunch supporter of the Free French of Charles de Gaulle, believing that France's capitulation in the Second World War was the result of France's submission to bourgeois attitudes. — Ed.

62   'Where are you fleeing ahead, imbeciles?' — Ed.

mation of the ideal of a well-structured, organic, and hierarchical State governed by a principle of authority. Here certain difficulties emerge with regard to the issue of from where this principle may draw its foundation and consecration. Obviously, it cannot come from below, from the *demos*,[63] which — *pace*[64] the Mazzinians[65] of yesterday and today — does not express the *vox Dei*[66] at all — if anything, the very opposite. One must also rule out dictatorial and 'Bonapartist' solutions, which can only be transiently valid, in emergency situations and under contingent, provisional terms.

Once again, we are forced to refer to dynastic continuity, provided — in the case of a monarchical regime — that what we have in mind is so-called 'authoritarian constitutionalism'. What this means is a kind of power that is not merely representative but also active and regulating on the level of 'decision-making' — as already discussed by de Maistre and Donoso Cortés with reference to ultimate decisions — with all the personal responsibilities this entails, when direct intervention is required because the present order has entered into crisis or new forces are looming on the political horizon.

Let us repeat, however, that the rejection of 'static conservatism' in such terms does not concern the sphere of principles. For the man of the Right, principles always constitute a solid foundation, a bedrock in

---

63 Ancient Greek: 'the common people of a state'. — Ed.

64 Latin: 'with the permission of'. — Ed.

65 Giuseppe Mazzini (1805–1872) was a philosopher and Italian nationalist who led a number of failed insurrections intended both to gain Italian independence from the Austrian Empire, and to unify Italy. Even once Italy began to gain actual independence in the 1860s, however, Mazzini still voluntarily remained in exile due to his disagreement with the favoured idea that Italy should become a kingdom, since he preferred a republic (which finally did become a reality in 1946). Despite his failures, Mazzini has always been hailed as one of the founders of the modern Italian state. — Ed.

66 Latin: 'the voice of God'. — Ed.

the face of change and contingency. Here the catchword must always be 'counter-revolution'. If we like, we may adopt the only apparently paradoxical formula of 'conservative revolution'. This concerns all those initiatives that are required in order to remove negative situations of the factual sort, which is a necessary step for restoration and for any suitable recovery of what possesses intrinsic value and cannot be called into question. Indeed, in conditions of crisis and subversion, nothing has a more revolutionary character than the recovery of such values. The ancient saying *usu vetera novant*[67] highlights precisely the same context: the kind of renewal which can achieve a recovery of what is 'ancient', namely the immutable heritage of Tradition.

With this, we believe that the stance of the man of the Right has been adequately clarified.

---

67   Latin: 'old things become new with use'. — Ed.

THE CULTURE
OF THE RIGHT

(1972)

It is rather fashionable nowadays to speak of a 'culture of the Right', yet it is difficult to avoid feeling that this is only a matter of circumstance. Given the progress made by the Right in the field of politics,[68] an attempt is being to complete its development by setting up a cultural component as well. This, however, poses a number of problems.

First of all, we ought to define what we mean by 'culture'. One could refer to either the creative field or that of ideas and doctrines. The creative field (that of literature, novels, theatre, etc.) resists all formulas: every genuine and valuable creation here essentially depends on the presence of a corresponding climate. The fallacy of tailor-made creativity or creativity on demand is shown, for instance, by the worthlessness of art in the context of so-called 'Marxist' art or 'socialist realism'.

It is in the second field — and its various domains — that the nature of a culture of the Right could and indeed should be defined. But

---

68 Evola is referring here to the contemporary success of the far-Right party MSI-DN, led by Giorgio Almirante. In the 1972 elections, the party had received 8.7 per cent of the total votes for the Chamber of Deputies and 9.2 per cent for the Senate. The year before, in southern Italian cities like Catania and Reggio Calabria, it had received over 20 per cent of the votes. — Ed.

aside from the circumstantial expression 'of the Right', in essence one should refer here to pre-existent intellectual and critical viewpoints, which would only have to be restored and developed further. An attack against Marxism, its historiography and methodology, would be predictable. There are few people who still adhere to the trite dogmas of Marxism; and if this ideology poses a threat today, it is not on the cultural level, but on the practical level of politics, where it must be faced not through argument but by means of resolute action.

What should be included in a culture of the Right is a critique of science and scientism, whose collusions with Marxism are well known. I myself have recently made a few valuable contributions to this critique:[69] the 'demythologisation' of science is an important task; from a wider perspective, it would also be necessary to measure the improvements science has brought on a material level against their counterpart: the spiritual ravaging wrought by the scientific worldview.

A more important field of study for a culture of the Right is that of historiography. It is a fact that in our country, history has — almost without exceptions — been written from an anti-traditional, liberal-Masonic, and more or less 'progressive' standpoint. Our so-called 'national history' is marked — and not merely in its most stereotypical forms — by the emphasis and glorification of what possessed a chiefly anti-traditional character: from the revolt of the city-states against imperial authority[70] to those aspects of the Risorgimento which most

---

69 An issue of *Roma* published some nine months earlier (11 November 1971) contained an article by Evola entitled 'La religion della scienza' (The Religion of Science). — Ed.

70 In the eleventh century, Milan led a battle of the Italian city-states for independence from the Holy Roman Empire which succeeded. As a result, by the twelfth century, the Italian city-states were independent political entities with a strong inclination toward republican forms of government. — Ed.

reflected the ideas of '89,[71] to Italian intervention in the First World War.[72] This applies not just to our 'national history' but to history in general.

In this respect, we sadly lack any precedents which could be developed further. Some people recently invoked the names of Machiavelli and Vico,[73] which are quite out of place in this context: the material they had at their disposal was far different from ours and rather limited. At most, it would be possible to borrow Vico's interpretation of history as a process of regression: the moving away from the level of what he called the 'heroic folk', towards new forms of barbarism. For Vico, however, all this falls within his theory of cycles, of historical transformation and return — and the same holds true in a way for the more up-to-date theories of Oswald Spengler and his *Decline of the West*.[74]

---

71 Following the independence of Italy from the Austrian Empire in 1861, the process of the unification of the Italian states into the Kingdom of Italy took place over the succeeding decades, and is termed the Risorgimento. Those such as Garibaldi and Mazzini, who led the Risorgimento, were strongly republican and democratic in their ideals. The 'ideals of '89' refers to the French Revolution of 1789. —Ed.

72 Upon the outbreak of the First World War, Italy at first maintained a neutral stance. In May 1915, however, despite the divided feelings of the Italian public, Italy entered the war on the side of the Triple Entente (the British Empire, France and Russia) against the Central Powers (Germany, Austria-Hungary, and the Ottoman Empire). Evola discusses all three of these cases at length in *Men among the Ruins*. — Ed.

73 Giambattista Vico (1668–1774) was an Italian philosopher who is best known for his book, *The New Science*, in which he outlined a cyclical theory of civilisations as progressing through three ages: the divine, the heroic, and the human age, which closely resembles traditional doctrines of history. — Ed.

74 Evola had earlier translated Spengler's work into Italian. In his introduction, which Evola also summarises in *The Path of Cinnabar* (London: Arktos Media, 2009), Evola praised Spengler for his dismissal of the linear, progressive notion of history in favour of a cyclical notion, but also criticised him for his lack of awareness of the transcendental aspects of culture and his embracing of several modernist ideas. — Ed.

As for Machiavelli, I really cannot see how he could contribute towards a historiography of the Right. More generally, we would like to voice some well-founded reservations concerning the attempt to class Machiavelli as one of the thinkers of the Right. After all, there is a reason why Machiavelli has given his name to 'Machiavellianism'. Even leaving aside the more unpleasant features of this theory — the unscrupulous use of any available means to achieve given ends — we are compelled to point out that we do not wish at all to associate the Right with the mere use of force, and with a form of power that resolutely affirms itself even when it is a shapeless power lacking any genuine foundation or a higher legitimacy. Otherwise, we would run the risk of having to accept quite a few contemporary regimes from behind the Iron Curtain.

The only valuable recent contribution towards an analysis of history from the Right — one capable of developing some of the suggestions found in Burke, de Tocqueville, de Maistre, and Burckhardt[75] — comes from Léon de Poncins and Emmanuel Malynski's book *The Occult War*, which has also been translated into Italian.[76] This work sheds light on the processes which — often unfolding behind the scenes of history as we know it — led to the disintegration of traditional society in Europe. Unfortunately, this investigation ends with the rise of Bolshevism. A rather large stretch of history — and a particularly eventful one — would thus have to be covered in order to reach the present day.

Another important field of study for the thought of the Right is that of sociology. For even when it is not pursued from an openly Marxist

---

75   Edmund Burke (author of *Reflections on the Revolution in France*), Alexis de Tocqueville (*Democracy in America*), Joseph de Maistre ('On the Pope'), and Jacob Burckhardt (*The Civilisation of the Renaissance in Italy*) are all well-known anti-liberal thinkers of the nineteenth century. — Ed.

76   *The Occult War* (Stockholm: Logik, 2015). The book was originally published in French in 1936. Evola translated it into Italian in 1939. The concept of the occult war became central to Evola's analysis of the modern world. — Ed.

angle, this discipline always contains a corrupting element: for it tends to equate the superior with the inferior without distinction, as the various currents of American sociology clearly illustrate. Finally, much attention should be paid to anthropology, understood as the general study of the human being. For instance, it would be necessary here to study and challenge the outlook — which unfortunately is so widely accepted nowadays — that serves as the premise for psychoanalysis (in all of its varieties), in such a way as to identify and challenge the partial and distorted idea of man that constitutes its general foundation.

With this, I believe, a few essential guidelines have been given.

HISTORIOGRAPHY OF THE RIGHT

(1973)

In developing some considerations regarding the European significance of Donoso Cortés, an interesting political figure and Spanish thinker who was active in the period of the first European revolutionary and socialist upheavals, a well-known German historian, Carl Schmitt,[77] noted that whereas Left-wing forces have systematically elaborated and perfected a historiography of their own as the general background for their destructive action, nothing of the sort has occurred in the opposite camp of the Right. Here all one finds are a few sporadic essays which are in no way comparable in terms of consistency, radicalism, and breadth of horizons to what Marxism and the Left have long possessed.

To a great extent, this is correct. Actually, the only kind of history that is known to the majority of people and which really counts, apart from that of Marxist tone, is essentially one of liberal, Enlightenment, and Masonic inspiration and origin. It draws upon those ideologies of

---

77 Carl Schmitt (1888–1985) was an important German jurist who wrote about political science, geopolitics and constitutional law. He was part of the Conservative Revolutionary movement of the Weimar era. He remains highly influential in the fields of law and philosophy. — Ed.

the Third Estate[78] which merely paved the way for the radical movements of the Left — having an essentially anti-traditional foundation
themselves. A historiography of the Right has yet to be written, and
this constitutes a point of inferiority for us with respect to the ideologies and disruptive action of the Left. In particular, this gap cannot
be filled by the so-called 'national history' of today: leaving aside the
nationalist veneer it may display and its moving commemoration of
given events and heroic figures, it too is largely influenced by a kind
of thought that is not of the true Right; even more importantly, this
historiography cannot be compared to that of the Left in terms of its
breadth of horizons.

Here lies the fundamental point. Ultimately, we must acknowledge
the fact that the historiography of the Left has been capable of focusing
on the essential dimensions of history: beyond all episodic conflicts
and political developments, beyond the history of individual countries,
it has successfully grasped the general and essential process which has
unfolded over the last centuries — namely, the transition from one type
of civilisation and society to another. The fact that this interpretation
rests on an economic and classist basis does not diminish the breadth
of the overall picture drawn by such a historiography. In examining
the course of history, the latter presents the end of the feudal and
aristocratic civilisation; the dawn of the bourgeois, capitalist, and
industrial civilisation; and the heralding and incipient accomplish-
ment of a socialist, Marxist, and finally Communist civilisation as the
essential reality beyond all contingent and particular realities. Here,
the natural causal and tactical linking together of the revolutions of
the Third Estate and those of the Fourth Estate are clearly recognised.
The idea of processes of a higher level being unwittingly favoured by
the more or less 'sacred' selfish interests of peoples, by the rivalries and

---

78 In pre-Revolutionary France, the general assembly of the French government
    was divided into three States-General: the clergy (First), the nobles (Second),
    and the commoners (Third). — Ed.

ambitions of men who believed they were 'making history' without ever leaving the field of the particular, is certainly taken into account. What is studied is precisely the overall transformation of the social structure and civilisation that is a direct consequence of the interplay of historical forces, whereas the history of nations is quite rightly relegated to the 'bourgeois' phase of general development. (Indeed, 'nations' only emerged as historical subjects with the revolution of the Third Estate, as one of its consequences.)

Compared to the historiography of the Left, that which reflects tendencies of a different sort therefore comes across as superficial, episodic, two-dimensional, and sometimes even frivolous. A historiography of the Right should embrace the same horizons as Marxist historiography. It should aspire to grasp the real and essential elements of the historical process which has unfolded over the last centuries, beyond all myths, superstructures, and even mere chronicles. This, of course, should be accomplished by inverting the signs and the perspective, in other words by seeing the essential and convergent processes of recent history as the phases not of any political and social progress but rather of a general subversion. Obviously, the materialist and economic premise must also be done away with, by acknowledging as mere fictions the *homo oeconomicus*[79] and inexorable determinism allegedly governing the various systems of production.

Much vaster, deeper, and more complex forces have been operating within history. With regard to particulars, the myth of so-called 'primordial Communism'[80] too must be rejected: in relation to the civilisations which preceded those of the feudal aristocratic type, this idea must be countered with that of forms of organisation chiefly based on a principle of pure, sacred, and traditional spiritual authority.

---

79   Latin: 'economic man'. — Ed.

80   Karl Marx and Friedrich Engels held that so-called 'primitive' societies were ordered according to a type of pre-ideological Communism, which came naturally to them. — Ed.

But apart from all this, let us stress once more that a historiography of the Right will acknowledge — as much as that of the Left — the succession and linking together of distinct general and supra-national phases, regressively leading up to the disorder and subversion of today. This will serve as the basis for an interpretation of individual facts and upheavals, one always focusing on the effect they have produced upon the overall picture.

Here it would be impossible to describe, even with a few examples, the fruitfulness of such a method and the unexpected light it would cast on a wide range of events: the political-religious conflicts of the imperial Middle Ages, the constant schismatic action of France, the relations between England and Europe, the true importance of the 'achievements' of the French Revolution, down to the episodes that especially interest us, such as the real nature of the revolt of the communes,[81] the double aspect of the Risorgimento as a national movement (triggered, however, by ideologies of the Third Estate), the significance of the Holy Alliance and the efforts of Metternich[82] — that last great European — and then of the First World War with the re-bounding action of its ideologies, the positive and negative aspects

---

81   The communes were city-states which retained a degree of independence from their rulers in the Holy Roman Empire. In the 1240s, some of the Italian communes sided with the Guelphs in the opposition of Pope Innocent IV to the Emperor, with great success. — Ed.

82   Prince Klemens Wenzel von Metternich (1773–1859) was an Austrian statesman who was one of the most important European diplomats of the nineteenth century. He was involved in the negotiation of the Treaty of Paris in 1814, which marked the end of the Napoleonic Wars. At the Congress of Vienna in 1815, he was instrumental in establishing the new map of Europe, which was to last more or less intact until the First World War, and the balance of power between Prussia, Austria, and Russia, known as the 'Holy Alliance'. Although he was generally a reactionary, he did believe that the Austro-Hungarian Empire needed to protect equal rights for all its ethnic groups, and even proposed the creation of a parliament to this end, but he was unable to enact such reforms. He was forced to resign during the Revolution of 1848. — Ed.

of the national revolutions accomplished not so long ago in Italy and Germany, and so on and so forth. Ultimately, we would get a view which corresponds to the naked reality of the true forces fighting for world leadership. This is only a selection of some intriguing topics among many others to which the historiography of the Right could be applied, so as to operate in an enlightening way and revolutionise the views held by most people regarding everything because of the influence of the historiography of the opposite orientation.

A historiography thus conceived, one looking to the universal, would be especially abreast of the times, if it is true that through irreversible objective processes we are now increasingly witnessing the emergence of fronts which are not simply comprised of particular, closed ethnic and political units. Unfortunately, the hoped-for historiography would only contribute to a heightened awareness. Given the current state of things, it could hardly also prove to be of practical effectiveness as a means of ensuring a decisive action, a relentless global fight against those forces which are about to sweep away what little remains of the true European tradition. Indeed, this would require, as a counterpart, a Right-wing international, as organised and powerful as the Communist one. Now, as is well-known, because of the lack of men of high stature and sufficient authority, of the predominance of partisan interests and petty ambitions, and of the lack of true principles and, not least, of intellectual courage, so far it has been impossible to establish a united Right-wing front even in Italy alone — only recently have initiatives of this sort been announced.

'NEUE SACHLICHKEIT':
THE CREDO OF THE NEW
GERMAN GENERATIONS

(1933)

In the preface to his notorious 'war novel', EM Remarque[83] writes, 'This book is to be neither an accusation nor a confession, and least of all an adventure, for death is not an adventure to those who stand face to face with it. It will try simply to tell of a generation of men who, even though they may have escaped shells, were destroyed by the war.'

Likewise, Prince Rohan[84] writes: 'Our generation has known no youth. Having entered the world tragedy as an adolescent, it came

---

83 Erich Maria Remarque (1898–1970) was a German writer who served as a soldier in the First World War. His most well-known work is his 1927 novel, *All Quiet on the Western Front*, which depicted the war as a horrific and futile struggle. — Ed.

84 Prince Karl Anton Rohan (1898–1975) was an Austrian First World War veteran, monarchist, and anti-modernist who later supported both Fascism and National Socialism, and hoped for a reconciliation between Christianity and the latter. He published his own *Europäische Revue* (European Review) from 1925 until 1936, which called for the creation of a new European identity in keeping with Europe's unique cultural and religious mission, and which would revive Europe's ancient values. — Ed.

out of it as a grave, lonely adult, bearing only the traces of the stern discipline of obeying and commanding.'

Nietzsche, prophetic as always, had already predicted the 'collapse of culture' and 'European nihilism'; but he had also written, 'Shaking a tree, only leaves that have already withered fall; what does not kill us makes us stronger.'[85] Just as the Book of Kings speaks of a light and pure breath 'which alone brings the Lord', after earthquakes and raging fire,[86] so Nietzsche had outlined the myth of a new race rising after its fall and embracing dazzling heights and supra-human realities once more.

Now, something of the sort is emerging in other countries, these writers' homelands. It is undoubtedly the case that, more than for any other race, for the races of the North the war has been a cause of destruction which is not only material but also, and primarily, spiritual. The soul of a generation has been shattered. This generation has found itself cut off from previous ones as if by an abyss: it no longer understands them — it stands apart from them. It lives a different life and does not even know what bridges have collapsed behind it. It is not a matter of new artistic or intellectual forms of expression, but rather of an inner change of attitude which has occurred almost independently of human will, as a state of affairs determined by the intrinsic force of things. Man's relationship with reality is no longer what it was; the very significance of what it means to be a man has changed. In Germany a

---

85   The first half of this passage has not been identified in Nietzsche's work, but the second (and much more famous) half is from Nietzsche's notebooks — specifically in this case, *Writings from the Late Notebooks* (Cambridge: Cambridge University Press, 2003), p. 188. — Ed.

86   In the King James Version of 1 Kings 19:11–12, the verses read: 'And he said, Go forth, and stand upon the mount before the Lord. And, behold, the Lord passed by, and a great and strong wind rent the mountains, and brake in pieces the rocks before the Lord; but the Lord was not in the wind: and after the wind an earthquake; but the Lord was not in the earthquake: And after the earthquake a fire; but the Lord was not in the fire: and after the fire a still small voice.' — Ed.

new, cold world is emerging; a free, anti-romantic world with no half-light or sentimentality: the world of the *neue Sachlichkeit,* the 'new spareness'.[87]

Neue Sachlichkeit is the catchword of a new Nordic youth.

* * *

In order to perceive to what extent this transformation affects all interests, all values, and all meanings of life, according to one central motif, one should read a recently published book which constitutes a bold and striking profession of faith by the new German generation. The author is twenty-seven-year-old Franz Matzke. The book is entitled *Confessions of Youth.*[88] What it presents is not a doctrine but a reality that some people may find disturbing and others unexpected; in any case, a reality that is indicative of the times to come.

> I will write about the meaning of life for the new generation, the unbroken among us, the Lords of tomorrow. There is a new race, with a new attitude of spirit and body, which is now rising up to fight, which will hold sway tomorrow, and wane the day after.

All footing has been removed, all bonds have been loosened, and all forces have been deprived of their objects: we have been left in the void, in complete relativity — Matzke states — and yet we have not fallen. We have fashioned a support and lifestyle for ourselves. We have not been overwhelmed by chaos but have attained a more lucid vision, a certainty regarding our condition. *And we have freed the world of reality from the world of human things.*

---

87 I prefer to translate *Sachlichkeit* as 'spareness' rather than 'objectivity'. *Sachlichkeit* comes from *Sache* = thing, not just in a material sense, but in the more general sense of a concrete, objective element ('to stick to the thing'). *Sachlich* describes what keeps to a given thing, to its essence, leaving out anything arbitrary, subjective, or accidental.

88 Franz Matzke, *Jugend bekennt sich: So sind wir!* (Leipzig: Reclam Verlag, 1930).

What distinguished previous generations, according to Matzke, was their worship of the 'soul'. In its name, they wrapped everything up in feelings, romantic undertones, a passionate warmth, tragic or intimate forms, and all sorts of 'intentions'. The naturalism of the last century[89] was nothing but a literary mask. At the centre of everything stood the human person with its problems, complexities, and judgements: the importance of everything was measured according to the extent to which it referred to such a centre. We wanted the world to speak of man, to take our form. So we infused the warmth of our own hearts into its starkness, we spiritualised it so as to reduce its distance and smooth its jagged edges: *Gefühl und Gemüt*.[90] We would never allow things to reach us directly: they were always expected to reach us through the 'soul'.

The new Nordic generation would appear to have scrapped all of this. The new generation tends to restore those qualities of eternity and indifference to the world with respect to human affairs which had been lost in previous epochs. It seeks to encounter things in all their starkness and harshness, silencing the soul and focusing exclusively on what is real: *neue Sachlichkeit*.

Matzke writes:

> We are *sachlich* because we are disgusted by everything which is merely human and speak of it as little as possible; because we see reality, which for us is higher than the thoughts of men — the reality of things is great and infinite, whereas everything human is small, conditioned, and

---

89 Naturalism was a literary movement. The authors who were part of it adopted an impersonal style, and attempted to approach subjects from a scientific, detached standpoint, explaining events in terms of natural laws instead of artistic, symbolic, or supernatural reasons. — Ed.

90 German: 'feeling and character'. *Gemüt* has an important meaning in the history of German philosophy; the German Idealist philosophers used it in the same sense that it had in medieval times, denoting a type of stable disposition of the soul which affects all of its faculties, directing them towards God. — Ed.

imbued with feeling. We are *sachlich* because objectivity, the absence of pretences and language in things, is closer to us than the loquacity of thoughts and passions; because only that which expresses itself in terms of reality interests us, and everything which is a direct expression flowing from heart to heart sickens us; because in every field we scorn authors' vanity, and place what is objective above all private psychology.

Thus, what we find first of all is the rejection of any compromise between things and men: an attempt to purify things from what is human, to restore the world as a serene, stable, clear, and stark place; to restore it to the magnificence of its first day, to its silent yet dazzling primordial greatness. No twilight glimmer, no muffling veil of illusions and thoughts: 'Better odious and bright than beautiful and dim.'

Matzke writes:

> Just as under the noon Sun, every bit of shade vanishes, so under our gaze things free themselves from the anaemic life of our fellow men, which had slipped into everything, weakening, distorting, and corrupting it: things regain their freedom and brightness. It is not that we have become insensible. If others wish to think that a soul which remains silent is no longer a soul, so be it: we too have a sensibility, only it is awakened not by other people's feelings, but by real things and what is most real and basic in man.

This is the heart of the *neue Sachlichkeit*. A change of attitude of this sort entails a shift of focus from one aspect of nature to another. These young generations are no longer interested in the picturesque, 'artistic', rare, and peculiar things nature has to offer. They no longer turn to nature in search of what is 'beautiful', of what sparks dreams and fills one with nostalgia. Beauty, for Matzke, is a name that applies to human endeavours, not nature: in his view, there are no landscapes 'more beautiful' than others, but only those which are more distant, more boundless, more serene, harsher, or colder than others.

> For us, nature is the great realm of things — of the kind of things which
> do not demand anything of us, which neither impose their presence
> on us nor require any particular attitude of our soul, but simply stand
> before us as a world unto itself, external and alien. This is exactly what
> we need, this greatness and distance, resting in itself, beyond all the
> petty joys and sorrows of man: a self-enclosed world of objects, in which
> we ourselves feel like objects. Completely detached from everything
> merely subjective, from every personal vanity and trifle: such is nature
> for us. We lack any inclination towards worship, so ours is no worship
> of nature. No God speaks to us through the landscape — no God and no
> man. And herein lies the greatness of the landscape, and our happiness.

It is no longer through picturesque waterfalls, sunsets, or moonlight
that nature speaks to the new generation, but through deserts, rocks,
steppes, glaciers, black Norwegian fjords, and scorching tropical
suns — through everything primordial, serene, inaccessible, and
silent. Matzke notes that the very form in which nature conveys its
significance has changed today: it is epic rather than lyrical, serene
and continuous rather than exceptional. The previous generation
would contemplate Alpine vistas or leaf through illustrations of them;
the new generation climbs walls of rock and frozen cliffs; the former
was driven to experience feelings by nature, the latter is driven to action; the former perceived things with its 'soul', the latter with its body.
Moreover, for the past bourgeois-romantic generation, nature was
like a lover one sees at the weekend or during the summer holidays:
a poetic interruption of city life. For the new generation, by contrast,
it is something fundamental, in the sense that it carries existence
within it something grave and hard: it is the great, vast world in which
metropolitan landscapes of stone and steel, with their endless linear
streets and building sites filled with forests of cranes, which stand on a
par with the immense and lonely forests — and the perception of their
austerity never leaves man.

Matzke writes:

In such a way, the *neue Sachlichkeit* forges an inner style, a posture of the spirit: just as we boycott sentimentality, so we lack both the drive and the joy to express ourselves and to 'communicate'. We feel a natural loathing for externalising what lies within us. We no longer enjoy speaking, and when we write, we state things rather than feelings. We keep to primordial states and emotions, avoiding any hypocrisy or emotional outburst through the objectivity of our attitude, the calmness of our being, and our love of distance.

This is another defining feature of the spirit of the new Nordic generation: the fact that it remains grave and reserved even in the midst of the crowds and commotion of the modern world, even within the inextricable fabric and demonic bustle of the big city:

We feel we are in a hard world, with no supports or guides. We rest on a gravity which is calm, natural, and simple — not the reflection of any internal or external worry. Silence and action are the distinguishing features of our style. We love impersonality, the vanishing of man before work or things. We appreciate the greatness of medieval anonymity, so free of personal vanity, whereby no one ever sought to convey the pain or joy in his heart, but serenely created his work. 'Tragedies' for us are merely a private matter, which only concern those who think themselves important. We are more inclined towards observation and action than sentimentality and emotional outbursts. For us youth of today, there is no God to whom we can speak about our suffering: the greater the pain, the more sealed our lips. The opposite behaviour would amount to pettiness for us, not greatness. Works no longer speak to us about their authors: they stand before us as closed and independent 'things', in a higher sense.

Thus, the 'human' warmth and closeness of former days is replaced by coldness and distance vis-à-vis things and people — but 'especially vis-à-vis people':

Objectivity rules out proximity and requires distance: in order to see, it is necessary to move away. Besides [Matzke repeats once again] we feel like a solitary breed, even when forming a mass; only, not according to yesterday's idea of solitude. This carried a painful, desperate, and romantic note, whereas our solitude is a perfectly natural condition. We are free from all vanity with regard to our 'self'; indeed, we hardly think about our self at all: we are happy to get together, we are not selfish, we accept hierarchies just like the generations before us, and we act — yet we feel alone. We feel that deep down we are not connected by any bridge, that all bonds have been severed, that as wayfarers on this Earth, we are all strangers although we follow the same route, even with respect to the things we love: our land, our friends, our women. Moreover, ours is not a forced solitude, filed with regret for things lost ιιι ίιlι ιlι lιι (ιιιyιιJ. We have never cherished any ideals we might regret. We remain serene in our condition, in our distance. It seems obvious and natural to us, like a law governing things. Individualism as a theory or religion of the self — the individualism so dear to those who came before us — is utterly foreign to us: it no longer speaks to us in any way. Even less is the self something profound and filled with mystery, mystique, and transcendence for us; rather, it is like a hard stone providing a firm footing.

Exterior life has been freed from the manifestations of the soul and any attempt to affirm the 'self' precisely because we have shifted and restricted the centre of life inwards. For this reason, outwardly we are probably far less individualistic, and far more prone to coming together and accepting submission, than the previous generations.

The author further clarifies this idea through a compelling simile:

Just as a shepherd will descend from the mountain when the village is in danger to join the villagers' ranks and fight, speak, and sing with them, only to return to his mountain when the enemy has been defeated — and thus find himself alone once more with the green meadows and dark forests, the rolling avalanches and blue skies — so our existence consists of both solitude and promptness to action. Getting organised for an ideal, for a spark of enthusiasm, is inconceivable to us; but we are ready to get organised for common action, for the attainment of a shared goal.

* * *

It is easy to foresee the consequences which an attitude of this sort might have in the different domains of life. All warmth silently withdraws to the centre; externally, everything becomes clearer, harder, and simpler, acquiring an almost frost-like or metallic shine. The heavens gradually drift away from the Earth.

Love, for instance, is downplayed:

> From the very fact that we are not constantly subject to the senses, but rather almost free with respect to them, it follows that sexual things no longer carry the significance and importance they had in the past. Erotic obsessions of the sort one finds in Freud or Weininger,[91] the expedients for arousal and morbid sinfulness typical of a certain kind of pre- and post-war literature, the romanticism of a unique, fatal passion and the drama of unrequited or betrayed love, are all things which we perceive as belonging to a generation we no longer understand. Here, too, an inner transformation has occurred, as a self-evident fact. We have acquired a new naturalness, a new frankness, a new 'objectivity'. Rather than the idea of the 'couple', what comes naturally to us is the idea of a man by a woman's side [der Herr neben der Dame]. Our girls are less dressed up and embellished, yet have preserved their femininity, even though they are not subject to the various forms of sentimentalism and the bourgeois and moral limits which were incumbent upon well-bred young women in the past. Moonlight love affairs mean nothing to us: in terms of form, even our heart has grown almost cold: no chatter, no gestures, no sentimentalism, no flings. It is not that love — sexual attraction between man and woman — is dead; it has changed form: it is no

---

91   Otto Weininger (1880–1903) was an Austrian Jewish philosopher who became a Christian, despised Judaism, and, because of his belief that he had failed to overcome the latter within himself, committed suicide. His primary work, *Sex and Character* (Bloomington: Indiana University Press, 2005), offers a theory of gender based on the idea that all individuals are composed of both male and female elements, with masculinity described as the genius' striving for absolute understanding, and femininity as obsession with sexuality and motherhood. References to Weininger abound in Evola's own work. — Ed.

longer the flickering, vermilion flame it used to be, but a bright, steady, and visible light. Outwardly it has lost all its distinguishing marks, so to speak — it is devoid of hypocrisy and complications. For yesterday's youth, the feeling of love was something heavenly and miraculous; today it strikes us as an everyday thing which cannot constitute the centre focus of any serious life. Woman no longer stands before us as an idol, but as our equal.

Besides, we know that not even woman can bridge our fundamental solitude. She is simply a life companion for us, possibly a close and trusted one, to whom we remain faithful even though we know that she may leave us one day; a companion to whom we are inwardly bound by unfathomable external powers; and although we may know a lot about her — as she does about us — in many respects, in terms of what is essential she is still a stranger to us. Whether being the way we are makes us any happier, we cannot tell. Besides, joy is something personal. We have lost some things and gained others. In any case, we feel neither sick nor *blasé*, and this is not a matter of vanity but of the very force of things.

We will now move on to provide an overview of the effectiveness of the *neue Sachlichkeit* in the various cultural domains. But first of all it is worth noting that it would be a mistake to regard this as an expression of mere materialism, or as a counterpart to the two-dimensional and anti-metaphysical American outlook. Externally, some similarities may be found, but their meaning is profoundly different. Unlike the American soul, the Nordic one is rooted in a tradition of inwardness which cannot simply be dismissed. The *neue Sachlichkeit*, it seems to us, consists not in the rejection of metaphysics but rather in the fact that the latter coincides with reality, creating a perfect balance between receptacle and content. This is almost a new Classicism, a new Doric paganism resurfacing under Nordic guise: one that is less harmonious and bright, perhaps, and sterner, graver, and more active, but which nonetheless has its own sealed, steel inwardness. And this has nothing to do with flat, practical-minded Anglo-Saxon simplification. The new Nordic generations appreciate the closed, unambiguous, and precise shape of a physical object not in materialistic terms, but rather as a symbol of spiritual composure. They reject the indefiniteness of sentimentality and emotional displays not out of aridness, but driven by the practical effectiveness of an ideal akin to the Classical one of *virtus*[92] — out of a desire for form, a yearning for what is powerful, clear, and simple. Matzke loves the world of technology, but as the expression of a 'will to adequateness' (*Wille zum Adäquaten*). He is as indifferent to machines in themselves as he might be toward a knife or fork: he appreciates the criterion of reducing the expenditure of energy to a minimum by taking the most direct route, but — once again — not for the love of convenience as much as out of a yearning for clarity and objectivity, and a loathing for anything which is superfluous, operates in a void, and constitutes an aimless drive.[93] Finally, this search for and appreciation of stark, non-human *Sachlichkeit* in nature and disgust for the earlier worship of inwardness and psychology do not reflect an attempt to establish a realist, postitivistic worship of matter; rather, they reflect a heightened sensitivity towards that which transcends the human level.

It is in the light of this that one is to understand the great act of renunciation which the new Nordic youth is set to undertake: the renunciation of belief.

---

92 Latin: 'manly, valorous, courageous'. — Ed.

93 Matzke notes how different this new attitude towards the world of machines is compared to the attitude of those who sung its praises and imagined it would pave the path to 'progress' (an outlook reflected by the *Excelsior* ballets, but also compared to those who, more recently, saw machines as apocalyptic monsters of sorts and as the cause of the fall of civilisation (myths à la *Metropolis*). Even with respect to machines, the attitude of the new generation is one of coldness and indifference. It makes use of them as natural things and does not lose its composure at the sight of the most amazing technological inventions any more than it does at the sight of a common fork or knife.

Do we affirm the existence of God? Do we deny it? Neither one or the other. These problems have lost all meaning for us: we no longer understand them, they are alien to us. We are neither devotees nor romantic denigrators of God — least of all 'free-thinkers'. We are not enemies of the Churches. All religions seem worthy to us, yet we have become equally estranged from all of them, as from the great metaphysical systems. We see both merely as works of art, which is to say as phases of historical reality. Everything for us rests in itself, all things are equally close and remote — blissfully alien and silent. We make our way among them, acting and contemplating. Our eyes turn this way and that, taking in all objects: regardless of whether our hearts are full of joy or sadness, pride or misery, we are always alone. We no longer feel that we are under the eyes of a Father, but rather on the naked Earth. Nothing speaks to us of God any longer, neither in joy nor in sorrow. We have lost God and faith in him — literally so. We may be accused of being spiritually impoverished: but can we really be called poor for the lack of something which we no longer need? We do not have a God, yet we are not without him, nor do we feel desacralised [*wir haben keinen Gott, aber sind weder gottlos noch entgöttert*].[94]

This phenomenon, a loss of all supports which nonetheless does not cause any real collapse, is also to be found in other domains. Just as the new Nordic generation is indifferent to all faiths, so it has little

---

94 It may be interesting to note that Matzke's love for *neue Sachlichkeit* leads him to appreciate — from the point of view of style — Catholicism more than Protestantism. In Catholicism — he observes — the private excitement of the soul in direct dialogue with 'God' plays little part. To be Catholic is to be part of a grand world army led by remote leaders. In Protestantism, everything is warm and *herzlich* [cordial]; in Catholicism, everything is cold and rigorous: it is the domain of order, of commanding and obeying, of stable forms and stark constructions. The soul here does not express itself in direct, sentimental ways, but rather speaks through things, through signs and symbols — in a *sachlich* fashion. Catholicism means distance; Protestantism closeness and intimacy. Naturally, the issue of the extent to which Catholics themselves may agree with this interpretation remains open, since it clearly appreciates the Roman-pagan component in Catholicism more than it does the original devotional and brotherly element of Christian zeal.

sensitivity toward or interest in philosophical constructions — unconsciously so, for it simply experiences this as an objective fact. The new generation no longer overestimates thought: it strips the 'thinker' of the kind of primacy and worship he had enjoyed in previous ages. It prefers to know that it does not know than to believe or speculate. This generation no longer understands the quest for the underlying 'meaning' or 'essence' of the world. Every 'cosmic synthesis' strikes it as cheap and pointless.

> Today we have a sense of certainty in life which does not stem from any metaphysical or religious justification. While we lack a transcendent background, we are neither overwhelmed nor afflicted by this: we act, think, and fight as much as those who had one and who needed to find a 'meaning' in life in order to live. For our action, we expect nothing whatsoever in return. The death of the gods has not turned us into epicureans or materialists or sceptics in a passive sense, nor has it turned us into apathetic ascetics or contemplatives. We like action and feel there is a lot to be done. We experience a kind of everyday heroism, with no fanfare, or romantic or titanic overtones. We love submitting ourselves to a duty or aim, to the point of self-effacement, but we need no support for this: ours is the ethics of the transoceanic pilot, of the sportsman, of the scientist — 'let the self perish as long as the object to which I am devoting myself is met'; it is also — and especially — the ethics of the good soldier, who does not enquire as to the 'ultimate meaning' or 'justification', and indeed expects nothing in return for what he is required to do, but simply acts, maintaining a strict, silent composure both outwardly and inwardly.

Matzke goes on to explain that the word 'progress', too, in its idealistic sense, has become utterly incomprehensible:

> Not only do we not believe in it, but we do not even know what it means. Certainly, we are witnessing 'progress' in specific practical domains, such as the operation of telephones and hospitals. We are working to promote this kind of progress as energetically as everyone else, if not more so, but do not imagine that because of this mankind is really mak-

ing any steps forward. Ours is no 'pessimism towards civilisation' — as though we believed in given ultimate values or goals but had discovered the impossibility of accomplishing them in contemporary reality, or even their inadequacy with respect to it. The very notion of such values is foreign to us, so it would make little sense to accuse us of 'pessimism'. Our actions are free: they occur in a pure, cold, and stark atmosphere. The very conception of the existence of 'culture' has acquired a different meaning: 'culture' for us is the expression of an inward attitude, the greatness of which is measured by its unity and self-containment — and what can this have to do with paintings, poems, or speculative enquiries? With the new generations, we are witnessing the emergence of a new meaning of life and action, yet not by virtue of any new 'culture' or philosophy. It fatally emerges not as a 'value', but as a state of affairs; and probably it will not even find any reflected or artistic expression, since 'expression' is no longer of any interest to the new generation: it is no longer an 'artistic' and 'expressionistic' generation.

By this route, the author once again broaches the crucial topic of the 'return to the great world'. He speaks of being sick of books and art and reveals the significance of a new enthusiasm for sport, something which does not exclusively apply to the young people he represents. Still, in this case too, it would be wrong to simply identify the new Nordic attitude with that which distinguishes American-style sport, for instance.

Matzke states:

> One difference when compared to the previous generation is that surrogates and transpositions of life have ceased to interest us more than life itself. What we are interested in is not that which shows through other people's feelings, but what shows through our own feelings, in the sunlight and open air. Yesterday's youth would read travel books; today's youth are travellers — and our travels are more 'epic' than 'lyrical'. Speed destroys the episodic, local, picturesque, and peculiar features of the lands we cross; it prevents us from developing any sentimental attachment towards them and awakens great, unitary, simplified, and universal feelings within us — the feeling of being world travellers, along

with that of power and safety in respect to things. We love sport not as trend or new religion, but because it releases these things from our soul, because it leads us from the realm of feelings to that of actions, into the cold, clear air: it is a language of things and bodies rather than souls. All we want is air — however icy and biting — and the harsh aspects of the world, unmitigated. We want to be wide awake — not dreamers who speak pretty words. Actually, we do not even 'want' this: simply, things could not be any other way.

So those claims, such as the statement that art is the highest human possibility, have become quite incomprehensible to us. We have become too serious, and art is no longer enough for this seriousness. We dispute everything which has been said about art as a means to reveal the essence of the world: these were pretty words, but they never found any real confirmation. Art is a fluttering about things, not a means to penetrate their core. 'Life is serious, art is lighthearted': we can once again appreciate the meaning of Schiller's words.[95]

From this it follows that in place of the blending of art and life, what is required is a clear-cut separation between the two: what is sought for, as already noted, is a perception of things without the mediation of the artistic soul of one's fellow man — the perception of things as great, remote, and independent of time and man. What is required is that things speak to man, and no longer that man speaks to things through his overflowing. At most — as in Schlegel — art is assigned value as a source of irony, as pure form: it is a thing unto itself, a separate thing.
Hence:

Today, we prefer to go out into the open air first and only afterwards into a library or museum, and then only if we still have time and feel like it. Should we call this progress or regress? We do not know — besides, these words are foreign to us. All we know is that things have changed and that we feel neither poorer nor unhappier than before. Today,

95	This is the final line of the Prologue of Schiller's 1798 play, *Wallenstein's Camp.* — Ed.

meaning in life comes only from factories and houses, not museums: it is swifter, clearer, more unitary. We feel at ease in cities, on rivers, and on peaks, not among books or in theatres. Above and around us is the real world — inexorable, great, soulless. Poems and paintings are only a tiny part of it. The world is great, but poems are short and paintings narrow. We cannot rank the work of man above that of God, and therefore we are 'without culture' (*kulturlos*) — the French are justified in calling us Germans 'barbarians'.

Even man's relationship with himself, which is to say with his 'soul', undergoes transformation in the direction of a *neue Sachlichkeit*. The love of introspection, inward reflection, and the analysis of one's thoughts and feelings pushed to the morbid limits so typically exemplified in the modern world, by the Russian novelists as well as Joyce and Proust, is something that the new generation completely ignores. It no longer views the soul from within, so to speak, but rather sees it from without, with detachment, as one might gaze at things in the external world under a bright light that sharply reveals their outlines. No emotional, literary, or mystical intermediary stands between awareness and its content. Hence, it is an attitude of sincerity and the destruction of all forms of individualistic narcissism, of all complications, of all masks. Matzke states:

> Ultimately, in our eyes, even the life of the soul amounts to a thing, to a fact, with the quality of being foreign, distant, and inevitable. More than gazing at the world from the soul, we gaze at the soul from the world. Then everything seems clearer, more natural, and more evident; and everything merely subjective increasingly strikes us as irrelevant and laughable, even when we silently experience the same passions, desires, suffering, and struggles which from other people have elicited the so-called great screams of tragic humanity. With regard to the manifestations of the inner creativity of men, what interests us is merely what they are capable of expressing, not through feelings but through things, with clarity, coldness, and objectivity [*Sachlichkeit*]. The form this takes is a great, stable, clear-cut, broad, and well-structured one which betrays

its creator's constructive will, as opposed to his private feelings; a form
that springs from the grand serenity and immobility of the world rather
than from the petty pains of the self: monolithic, elementary, harsh, and
monumental.

* * *

These last words once again evoke the theme of a sort of reborn
Classical will. And we believe that this is precisely what constitutes
the positive aspect of the *neue Sachclickeit*, not least by comparison to
other trends which are stirring alongside the one whose spirit we have
become acquainted with through Matzkes' words.

Beyond the 'doom of the gods', beyond the flare of the war and the
miseries of its aftermath, what emerges under the guise of an extreme,
harsh modernity is the spirit of a new, activist paganism.[96] Its setting
is no longer Mediterranean temples, sun-drenched Ionian isles, or
the bright countryside of Latium, but rather a new world shaped by
the dynamism of machines, in which a strange new architecture has
sprung up where romantic, misty Nibelungian forests once stood, utterly erasing the Gothic spirit through harsh rectilinearity and rational,
clear-cut shapes consisting of glass and metal more than brick — as-
cetically stark and austere. It no longer reflects youth and joy, but the
gravity of life, matured under steel helmets, just as it once did under
the monastic cowl. It is no longer epic in a Pindaric[97] sense: it finds
expression not in games, competitions, and aerial dances, but on the
stage of the great world of things, on oceans, on silent, frozen peaks,
in deserts, in shiny wind-chasing machines, and in Nordic interiors

---

96 Here we have refrained from indicating which broader currents in the modern
    world may be seen to express the same drive as the new German generation
    which finds a profession of faith in Matzke's book. I will here refer to my essay
    'Superamento del Romanticismo' in issues 1 and 2 of the 1931 edition of *Vita
    Nova*.

97 Pindar (522–443 BCE) was an ancient Greek poet. Much of his work was cel-
    ebratory of achievements in athletic or musical competitions. — Ed.

stripped of all decoration — stark and clinical to the point of acquiring an archaic bleakness. It is free of any trace of melancholy or escapist nostalgia. 'What does not kill us makes us stronger; that which is not consumed, regains its purity.'[98]

An age has come to a close: the Romantic age. Fire has destroyed all the outer shells and exposed the essence of things. Outside Germany, another race has undergone this process: Russia. There, too, there is a *neue Sachlichkeit*. There, too, there is a desire to do away with the soul and the self, seen as 'prejudices of the bourgeois age'. There, too, anything subjective, arbitrary, personal, ideological, or sentimental is regarded as an irrational and baleful outgrowth, which suitable processes of rationalisation and mechanisation organised by the omnipotent state will make sure to root out. There, too, there is a yearning towards an impersonal world, a world of things more than men — a primordial, stark, and heavenless world. But the kind of *neue Sachlichkeit* which has come to light in Russia, with its undermining of established superstructures, is the ancient barbarian soul of the Slavic race, finally freed from the attempt to impose European civilisation upon it which the Czars had been undertaking over the past two centuries. This is the race of faceless men, the 'nameless beast', the headless but many-limbed 'collective man' embodied by an economic mechanism, in whose name all those who believe in 'Soviet civilisation' have sacrificed and forever destroyed everything that made them distinct and independent.[99]

What is emerging in Germany, instead, is the closed sense of the self which distinguishes an ancient warrior paganism, whose symbol today is evoked within Hitler's ranks by the black hooked Cross, a symbol of self-igniting fire and of the rising Sun — a symbol which Christendom

---

98 Again, the first half is the same as in the earlier reference, but the second has not been identified in Nietzsche's work. — Ed.

99 On this view of Soviet Russia, see our essay 'Americanism and Bolshevism' in *Nuova Antologia*, no. 10 (1 May), 1928.

never really vanquished in the feudal Middle Ages and which finally resurfaced, albeit through intellectual surrogates, in the great Idealistic philosophies. This sense of the self has now re-emerged in a simplified, metallic form as the core of the Nordic *neue Sachlichkeit*, and is being displayed as something simple and inalienable, even where the demon of cosmopolitan civilisation reigns.

What will be the future of these new generations? For what age are they heralding and paving the way? What will its meaning be for Europe and its tradition, which is currently threatened by a double peril, Russia to the east and America to the west?

The answer to these questions can only come from the future — a very near future, perhaps. Matzke writes, 'We know that we are nothing but a wave in a current with neither beginning nor end, and whose swift flow constitutes its very essence. Yet this wave — our wave — is the highest one now. We are moving towards a peak which for the moment is only surrounded by valleys.'

FOR A 'YOUTH CHARTER'

(1951)

The democratic representatives of defeat and treason have long been appealing to the Italian youth in a more or less pathetic and paternalistic way, seeking to make them follow their lead and win them over to their ideologies.

These fellows should realise that they are wasting their time. The Italian youth — the *true* Italian youth — have no need of them. They have a character and form of their own, and are increasingly aware of the political role they play — and will play — in the life of the country, in terms of the rejection of the moral condition that was created as a result of the unsuccessful war, as well as of a revolt against the renewed climate of an Italy ruled by petty politicians, stripped of its dignity and virility, and subservient to foreign interests.

Therefore, it is necessary for the Italian youth to lend clear expression to this revolt through an ideology and programme, so as to ever more broadly and consciously combine their forces and confidently progress along their path.

We wish to share the following notes with our friends and comrades. They are simply conceived as a starting point for the formulation of a *Youth Charter* to be approved by a national congress, on the one hand as a profession of faith free from all ambiguity or wavering and, on the other, as a means of action for the broad coordination of the forces of the new Italian generations, or at any rate the most vital ones.

YOUTH

1. We conceive youth not as a matter of age or a biological fact, but essentially as a spiritual attitude, as a *tone* and *style* of life. It is defined by the enthusiasm and generosity of those who follow an ideal simply out of love for this ideal; by a yearning for the unconditional, which is inseparable from any idealism; by a taste for action; by an impulse towards renovation, towards marching forward; by contempt for easy living.

2. Youth has a revolutionary character, where revolution is understood not as an inordinate desire for what is new and different or as a subversive force, but rather as intolerance for stagnation, a yearning to ensure the perennial relevance of one's ideal, and as a constant fire destroying all inertia and overcoming all obstacles.

3. Youth — *our* youth — therefore show themselves through a spiritual, heroic, and agonistic view of life. They reject all forms of materialism, all economic or socialistic myths, in all domains. It sees Americanism and Bolshevism as two sides of the same illness — not as two possible options. To both it thus opposes the right and value of a dominating personality, beyond the world of matter and quantity, of mercantilism and collectivism.

From this inner form of youth, the following political corollaries are derived:

INDIVIDUAL, STATE, NATION

1. We completely reject the myth of 'immortal principles',[100] along with all that is based on them. To the atomistic, egalitarian, and libertarian concept of the *individual*, we oppose the differentiated and qualitative one of *person*, understood as a dignity that is not given to everyone but must be earned, and which — even when it has been earned — is not the same for everybody. The inseparable counterpart to this is *hierarchy*.

2. We conceive the state as a super-naturalistic order within which the values of one's personality are integrated and each human activity, arranged according to a system of disciplines, may acquire a higher significance. The state must never degenerate into a cold and impersonal entity, into a levelling legal abstraction. The state must be made up of men and leaders of men. *Authority*, conceived first of all as spiritual authority, is the basis of the true state — *our* state. At the same time, authority means *power*.

3. Freedom, in the true state, must be conceived not in individualistic and democratic terms, but rather in relation to its specific function within an organic system. The true freedom is not that of the abstract 'rights' of natural law theory, but rather that which is exercised through relations of obedience and command — of spontaneous obedience and responsible command.

4. The nation develops from being a naturalistic reality defined by ethnic, territorial, and linguistic factors, or an association of citizens, into a spiritual fact when it is integrated within the state. The state represents the higher conscience of the nation, manifesting itself within it as an idea and power.

---

100 How the principles of the French Revolution were sometimes referred to, one of the slogans of which was 'liberty, equality, brotherhood'. — Ed.

CULTURE, SOCIETY

1. Both the liberal concept of culture and the simply humanist or aestheticising one are quite foreign to the youth — the new or, at any rate, more lively generations. They primarily conceive of culture in classical terms, as being synonymous with style: one's inner style. In the climate of this difficult age, they no longer value mere bourgeois art and disorderly, subjective creativity that is detached from all principles and shows no character or uprightness. The heroic view of life goes hand-in-hand with a realism that sets clear limits upon the previous worship of the 'intellectual'.

2. Precisely in the name of its heroic and anti-materialistic conception of life, the youth equally oppose the widespread mental distortion which places every human activity into the category of 'labour'. As in all normal civilisations, the term 'labour' must be limited to the more materially conditioned, and hence subordinated, forms of human activity. The higher expressions of human personality must be defined not in terms of 'labour', but in terms of *action*. Against the tendency to degrade every action by conceiving it as a form of 'labour', one must rather affirm the need to elevate labour by conceiving it, whenever possible, as a form of action. Neither the 'state of labour' — strictly speaking — nor the 'humanism of labour',[101] both of which betray a proletarianised view of life, can fulfil our ideal. This ideal — let us stress once more — is chiefly a heroic one. It is above the world of labour and production (the last

---

101 Giovanni Gentile, who was an Idealist philosopher who was known as the 'philosopher of Fascism', coined this term in his posthumously published book (he had been assassinated by anti-Fascist partisans in 1944), *Genesis and Structure of Society* (Urbana: University of Illinois Press, 1960). It sought to synthesise socialist ideals with nationalism, as was attempted in the Italian Social Republic that existed in northern Italy from 1943 until 1945. Evola strongly disagreed with the socialist elements of the Republic's ideology. — Ed.

words for Bolshevism as much as Americanism) that it finds the highest forms of interest and modes of personal realisation.

3. The *family* is among the values to be defended both against Communism and against the liberal-atomistic conception of the individual. Yet in order to promote and protect it from the process of dissolution now well underway, it must be 'de-bourgeoisised' and integrated with the concepts of folk and tradition — those of the blood as much as of the spirit. Only then, once the family has ceased to be a mere naturalistic and conformist reality, can its order be organically restored within the state, thereby confirming the hierarchy of values under mortal threat by self-serving democratic and liberal conceptions.

4. The youth conceive the party system and democratic representation as resurgences of the past, as an outdated system whose incapacity to face current problems is increasingly evident, especially in Italy. The Italian youth feel the need for a corporative system of representation, which takes the specific form of *categories of value* and hierarchies of competences: all this, outside of any party or cabal, within an organic system that finds its centre in a superior principle of authority, the purely political principle which stands as the basis of the true state.

ITALY, EUROPE

1. The youth want Italy to regain its dignity and confirm its inseparable unity; it wants suitable, energetic, and resolute men to proudly proclaim the country's rights before foreign powers and the new supra-national blocs of East and West, by adamantly refusing to follow those who — in the name of a defeat for which not our, but their own deceit is to be blamed — wish to brand both Italy and ourselves with the mark of servitude, or at any rate of perpetual subordination.

2. However, given the power of the competing world forces and inter-
    ests, the youth look towards the establishment of a bloc of European
    states on a national basis, as the expression of a new generation and
    of a reborn, august tradition that extends through the centuries all
    the way back to Rome. Consequently, there is no plan to achieve
    artificial unity through a feeble and inefficient 'European federal
    parliament'. Here too, the idea is that of an organic, virile, and
    hierarchical unity to which each European country may contribute
    with its own genius, while preserving its own individuality and
    rightful place.

3. Within this framework, Italy may serve a higher mission not so
    much as a 'Latin' nation, but as a *Roman* one; and this, to the extent
    that, as the most adequate means for reacting against the current
    climate of moral, political, and social disintegration in our country,
    it will prove capable of drawing upon those elements of style and
    uprightness that shaped the Roman man and, later, the man of the
    Romano-Germanic European civilisation.

THE ACTION OF THE ITALIAN YOUTH

In accordance with these guidelines, the Italian youth seek to establish
a spiritual and national movement that — in order to train the cadres
of a new ruling class constituting an 'order of believers and fighters' — will pursue the following goals:

A. To steer the youth as a whole: to detoxify those sections of it that
    have fallen under the spell of either Left-wing currents or of the
    'democracy' now in vogue; to take a stand against those decaying
    and degenerate agonistic elements that live from hand to mouth
    and know nothing more interesting than sport, dancing, and films.

B. To spark a new awareness, in universities as well as workplaces and clubs, by supporting and integrating the explicitly political action of the party.

C. To heighten the feeling of profound, existential detachment between the current ruling class and a lively, young, and revolutionary force that follows its own path and from which a new Italy and a new world will spring forth and affirm themselves.

D. To establish and develop contacts with the young, or at any rate most lively elements, in other European countries so as to ensure an appropriate coordination of the goals and the means to attain them.

E. To provide a distinctive contribution to the political battle being waged by the MSI, to which the youth is offering its solidarity, trusting it will not be disappointed. This contribution will take the concrete form of doctrinal intransigence and of a rigorously pure Ideal, made possible by the fewer constraints imposed upon a youth that is to present themselves chiefly as a spiritual movement.

BIOLOGICAL YOUTHFULNESS AND POLITICAL YOUTHFULNESS

(1974)

One of the questions which frequently crops up in Right-wing milieus is that of the new generation and its relations with the previous one — in other words, the question of the 'revolutionary' youth and its relations with the men and ideas of the Fascist period. Some people believe that it is possible to detect here something which may also be observed at a more general level: the new generation no longer understands the previous one, since the accelerated unfolding of events has created a distance between the two in terms of ideals greater than the one which would normally have separated them.

However, this perspective often betrays a certain superficiality and bias. Besides, are the concepts of 'youthfulness', new generation, and 'revolutionary vocation' not rather ambiguous ones?

Indeed, it is worth defining the level on which we wish to apply such notions: whether this is the biological level or instead a higher one, as in our case one ought to suppose. If we wish to consider things in spiritual terms, we must be cautious, since in some cases certain values can become inverted, when it comes to the meaning to be assigned to that which is 'new', young, and most recent. Thus, generally speaking, if we consider the generations that follow one another within a specific cycle of civilisation, in the aforementioned cases one may even speak of a paradox: for youthfulness is to be assigned to that which stands at the origins, whereas the last, chronologically younger generations are the older, senescent, twilight ones — even though infantilism and primitivism may at times be mistaken for youthfulness. To mention just one example, the so-called 'youthfulness' of the North American racial types, with their 'new world' and primitivism, may clearly be seen to reflect the infantilism which distinguishes not 'young' genera- tions, but the last generations, the regressed ones found towards the end of a cycle — the cycle of Western civilisation in general.

Mention has been made of this because something similar holds true in a more concrete domain. Let's take a look around us: can we really call a fair share of the 'youth' in contemporary Italy 'young', other than merely biological terms and date of birth? This indifferent and agnostic youth, in the grips of materialism and petty hedonism, is in- capable of any real drive or conduct — the closest it comes to display- ing any trace of liveliness is at football matches and the Giro d'Italia.[102] We might say that this youth has died even before being born. Anyone today who does not give in, who lives according to an ideal, who is capable of firmly keeping his stand, and who despises all that is feeble, devious, twisted, and vile, whatever his age, is infinitely 'younger' than the particular 'youth' in question.

It is precisely according to these terms that we are to understand what constitutes youthfulness in more than the merely biological sense and to define a common denominator transcending artificial antith- eses. If I were to pinpoint the distinguishing feature of youthfulness, understood in this higher sense, I would refer to the *will toward being unconditioned.* This factor may be seen to underlie, on the one hand,

---

102 An annual bicycle race in Italy. — Ed.

all idealism in the positive sense, and on the other, any courage, drive, creative initiative, or tendency to resolutely take up new positions with little concern for one's own person. In particular, in physical terms, authentic youthfulness displays the almost paradoxical disposition typical of a flourishing life which, instead of showing self-attachment, is capable of unhesitatingly sacrificing itself, to the point of defying death.

It is worth drawing a distinction between the more elementary phase, in which the qualities just mentioned only manifest themselves in a spontaneous, disorderly, and transient manner, often like a flash in the pan, and the phase in which they have been confirmed and stabilised. The former is frequently the case with actual young people, who then gradually 'settle down', 'get their act together', and become persuaded that 'idealism is one thing, life another', thereby relinquishing their will to unconditioning, which turns out to have largely rested on a physical basis. The latter case, instead, is that of someone who has faced some challenges, some difficult challenges, and overcome these challenges without ever giving in.

This applies to the inner domain as much as the political one — which brings us back to the problem we started with. Which generation of yesterday would today's generation struggle to understand? Ultimately, what we witness is a return: for yesterday, too (i.e., in the aftermath of the First World War), there was a 'generation of the front'; and, likewise, intolerable political, social, and moral conditions fostered a kind of defiance, idealism, and virility which found expression in a life of danger and fighting — the premises of the Fascist movement. Much the same situation has emerged today, with the addition of the aggravating circumstance of a more difficult challenge, since what the 'generation of the front' has experienced is not a victory, but a defeat and general collapse.

A fundamental continuity ought to exist in this respect. This continuity, represented by political rather than biological 'youthfulness', does not apply to the men of yesterday who lost themselves when Fascism came to power, who failed to preserve their integrity, their will to being unconditioned, and their radicalism, selling their birthright for a dish of pottage:[103] for this or that semi-bureaucratic office in the framework of a despicable, hollow 'hierarchism' and new conformism.

Still, it would be unjust to throw the baby out with the bathwater[104] and fail to acknowledge that the Fascist ranks also included men who stood their ground, often against the opposition of this or that officious clique. Their uniting with the new wave, with the new youth and new 'generation of the front,' ought to be a natural development and a matter of congeniality: like a current which resumes its course after overcoming an obstruction, a blockage.

Let us mention another point. It is not always easy — particularly in the case of Italians or Mediterraneans — to see oneself as having independent value. In order to perceive their individuality, their importance, many people feel the need to get all worked up, to pit themselves against something or someone. It is in light of this that we must judge certain aspects of the 'revolutionary vocation' and of a certain kind of individualism displayed by the 'youth', who seek to distinguish themselves at any cost and to indiscriminately endorse new ideas, simply because of their novelty. What often lies at the basis of all this is simply an 'inferiority complex': the need to assert one's worth in an indirect way, by antithesis and contrast, since one is not sufficiently self-confident. This is an attitude which the political youth, as opposed to the merely biological youth, ought to rectify. The highest ambition should not be to assume the role of revolutionaries at any cost, but

---

103 Genesis 25:33–34: 'And Jacob said, Swear to me this day; and he sware unto him: and he sold his birthright unto Jacob. Then Jacob gave Esau bread and pottage of lentiles; and he did eat and drink, and rose up, and went his way: thus Esau despised his birthright.' — Ed.

104 The Italian saying Evola uses is 'to make a single bundle of all the grass', with fascio meaning bundle — undoubtedly a deliberate play on words. — Ed.

rather to stand as the exponents of a tradition, as the harbingers of a transmitted power which must be increased by any means which might lend it an inflexible direction. This also concerns the domain of ideas: one of the proofs of inner freshness is to be found in the fact that right ideas overcome all contingencies and lend value to one's authentic personality — not through a confused revolutionary instinct, a prejudiced suspicion of the past, or a disorderly dynamism which simply betrays the lack of any authentic inner form. Without wishing to reach any particular conclusions — for this is not the appropriate venue — it should be easy to see which aspects of the general attitude of today's political youth are to be rectified in order to join forces and pursue a well-defined political ideal: the ideal of the authentic organic state.

GOLIARDISMO AND YOUTH

(1955)

A few days ago, on the Italian radio, we happened to hear about a small survey concerning *goliardismo*[105] that was carried out by a sort of magazine apparently run by young people. We later discovered its title — *Primavera*. The survey was also conducted by young people, who were the concerned party. One of the guest speakers was presented as bearing the title of 'Prince of Italian *goliardia*'.

What we have heard calls for a few brief considerations. First of all, we should note a rather inopportune and altogether distasteful political suggestion that was advanced. One of the speakers claimed that the attitude of the *goliardi* has always stood in opposition to Fascism since, as non-conformists, they could never accept totalitarianism; and that, besides, Fascism opposed all expressions of *goliardismo*.

What this judgement betrays is precisely a foolish conformism (to the ideas en vogue nowadays, even in the absence of 'totalitarianism') on the part of someone who, as a *goliardo*, claims to be a nonconformist. In any case, the fact that the judgement in question is a

---

105 The term *goliardia* refers to student associations that are similar to the fraternities one finds in the United States, but are differentiated by the fact that, being hundreds of years old, they have many more traditions that are maintained, and members often don medieval garb for official ceremonies. As in other types of fraternities, pranks are a major part of the life of *goliardi*, especially those which are played on the newer members. — Ed.

biased one is shown by young people's contribution to early Fascism. Before being adopted by the Arditi,[106] the Fascist hymn *Giovinezza* was originally a goliardic hymn. And this is not to mention the young university students who later joined the Fascist wars as volunteers, sacrificing their lives *en masse*.

Just to what extent Fascism and totalitarianism may be seen to coincide is an issue we shall leave aside.[107] Certainly, in some ways totalitarianism might be described as 'the regime of nuisances' on account of the impertinent interference that the public authorities have in the private sphere. Its centre lies not in the natural authority of a genuine elite, but in a form of imposition worthy of a corporal or cane-wielding pedagogue: among craven souls and spineless men, it therefore takes the form of a school of conformism. Defiance against such a system is hardly the privilege of *goliardismo*. But it is precisely here where one is led to wonder what *goliardismo* actually means.

It is said: it is an expression of youth, mirth, and light-heartedness. But having been students ourselves, of course, back in the day, before Fascism, we would say that unruliness, rowdiness, and superficiality play a greater part, in addition to the ostentatious and carnivalesque grotesqueness that distinguishes certain 'traditions'. Besides, not all youth are the same, nor should we be under any illusions about what simply represents an outlet for the kind of excess vitality typical of the age in which the powers of sex awaken without finding adequate satisfaction. In our own youth, we took part in various student events, including ones with political overtones, starting with pro-war rallies. A keen eye would hardly miss the fact that what mattered was finding a release for the aforementioned exuberance — the rest being merely an excuse. On these bases, it is also possible to argue that goliardic defiance amounts to defiance as a matter of principle, verging on sheer

---

106 The Arditi were the shock troops of the Italian army during the First World War. — Ed.

107 Evola addresses this issue in *Fascism Viewed from the Right*. — Ed.

indiscipline; and that non-conformism also has this character, when it is genuinely to be found, beyond any exterior and largely insignificant gestures. We should add that, on account of the general sapping of their vital drive, today's youth strike us as being far less non-conformist than those of the past. Besides, Fascism offered far more effective and serious means to channel excess vitality.

In the conversation to which we have referred, concerning some recent goliardic events — held in Rome, if we are not mistaken — one of the speakers mentioned the forced, contrived and — for many people — annoying character of what was at first perceived as youthful mirth. Another speaker spoke of the decadence of the goliardic traditions — compared to what, we really could not tell, without delving into history. For, as far we can recall, a couple of decades ago the situation was much the same, with freshers' parties, rowdy meetings, jokes and pranks, and so on. Someone added that in the past, *goliardismo* found its symbol in *Addio Giovinezza*[108] (the comedy and operetta): this would shift everything to a rather disintegrated and stereotypical romantic-sentimental level.

One is led to wonder whether in these aspects of *goliardismo* race might come into play — in our case, the 'Mediterranean' race. This is suggested by a comparison with the old goliardic corporations in Germany, particularly those known as *Korps-Studenten*.[109] The excess vitality of youth was here expressed through traditions more worthy of such a name. Truly non-conformist revelries were not absent

---

108 *Goodbye Youth* was a play written by Nino Oxilia and Sandro Camasioin 1911, which was later adapted into several films. The story is about a student from Turin who first falls in love with a seamstress, but is then seduced away by an older woman. — Ed.

109 The German student corporations are similar to fraternities in the United States, but traditionally were much more military in structure and comportment, such as in the wearing of uniforms. — Ed.

(the young Bismarck providing a notable example in this respect).[110] Sometimes, they would take the form of a test: in certain cases, in order to be accepted by the elders, the 'freshman' was required not to lose his head and to sharply reason about philosophy or theology after very intense drinking bouts. But what was more interesting in these groups was their spontaneous enthusiasm for military attire, and their ideas of fraternal honour and courage, which were often carried to extremes. According to the *Mensur* tradition, in order to become a truly accredited member of the corporation, the *Korps-Student* was required to stand his ground in special fencing duels, with only the non-vital parts of his face exposed. The scars visible on the face of Germans of the past generation from the non-proletarian classes are reminders of their goliardic days.

In our own country, the maximum limit would appear to be constituted by some burlesque feats involving the kidnapping of the 'prince' of *goliardia* of one city by that of another city, followed by retaliation: amusing deeds, perhaps, but nothing more. Besides, if we exclude sports, films, and dancing, it is difficult to tell just what is left in the Italian youth of today, both goliardic and non-goliardic. The only exception is represented by those youths who are truly non-conformist on a serious level and who nowadays belong to the national front. They are indifferent to organised misunderstanding and possible forms of persecution. Naturally, the speakers on the RAI[111] programme avoided mentioning them at all.

---

110 Bismarck was quite wild during his student days, leading to several appearances before the university's court for problems with the authorities. — Ed.

111 Radiotelevisione italiana is the public broadcasting corporation of Italy. — Ed.

THE YOUTH OF YESTERDAY AND THE TEDDY BOYS OF TODAY

(1958)

Little survives of the student traditions and organisations of the past. The goliardic customs and practices we personally remember from our own university days were essentially limited to a playful, careful, and carnivalesque youthful exuberance. At most, they took on a sentimental veneer, reminiscent of *Addio Giovinezza*. Things should not be all that different nowadays. We have heard about 'wars' waged by student groups from different cities. Last year, in Bologna, the resumption of some traditional student exploits and the freedom they entail were apparently the object of alarmed complaints from conformists.

In any case, these are nothing but faded residues. And it may be of interest to refer to some specific forms acquired by student organisations in other ages and countries. We should begin with the period in which the major European universities were founded, namely the late Middle Ages. Back then, knowledge did not have the popular character it has now: it represented something qualitative and exclusive. The same was true of pursuing any studies or belonging to a university.

It is well known that the age in question was one of guilds and orders. What existed were not standardised 'economic classes', but closed, differentiated, and organic bodies and associations that brought individuals together on the basis of a shared vocation or activity — in relation not just to one's trade or the pursuit of material interests, but to one's life as a whole. Thus, each of these guilds had its own principles, underlying spirit, 'honour', and ethic.

Even university students spontaneously organised themselves in this manner. Like many guilds made up of 'freemen', they often enjoyed special exemptions and privileges. Strictly speaking, even today the police would not have the right to enter universities: an echo of the fact that those student bodies did not fall under the ordinary jurisdiction, and thus their members could not be persecuted on their own turf. As a consequence of the principle of *ius singulare*[112] then in force — which is to say, a right not applying to all — university students could afford to do certain things which were off limits to ordinary burghers. Like the nobles, they could fight in a duel. Like many guilds or corporations, they had their own distinctive attire — remnants of which also survive, as in the case of the caps worn by the members of certain student groups.

In modern times, the area in which these traditions have been preserved the longest and in the most interesting forms is Central and Northern Europe, which is indeed the area which up until a few years ago best resisted the general process of democratisation. The ancient guilds, first abolished in France with the Jacobin revolution, soon lost their legal status elsewhere as well. In the above-mentioned area, however, they at least survived in spirit. In countries such as Germany, Sweden, Austria, and Denmark, students continued to form bodies

---

112 Latin: 'singular law', which is a type of law reserved for a specific group or type. — Ed.

that enjoyed special privileges, cherished their prerogatives and traditions, and abided by a code of their own, almost like a separate caste.

It is these offshoots that are worth referring to. It seems as though nothing of the sort ever had much following in the Latin countries, and especially in Italy, where the humanistic approach spread early on, along with municipal and bourgeois tendencies. By contrast, in the above-mentioned area the university milieu itself long continued to reflect the lifestyle and outlook of the feudal world.

Hence, the distinctive phenomenon of the so-called *Korpsstudenten*. These were very closed university organisations which, as a reaction to the idea of the student as someone buried in books and focused merely on absorbing 'culture', adopted a military style and a special code of 'honour' in contrast to the conduct of the bourgeois or the man in the street. In order to join these corporations, one had to go through a sort of initiation that was of a rather different sort from today's jocular rites of matriculation. Each new member would be assigned an elder to whom absolute obedience was due and who would make him undergo various tests, not all of them of an irreproachable sort. These included giving oneself over to excesses, particularly in drinking, without losing one's style of conduct and self-control. The Iron Chancellor, Bismarck, was particularly renowned in this regard. Anyone who did not live up to the challenge was regarded as not being 'man' enough to become a *Korpsstudent*. What was even more important, however, was displaying one's virility by engaging in duels, to the point of bearing scars on one's face from them. This was known as *Mensur*: fencing matches in which the vital parts of the duellist's body would be protected, but his face partly exposed. The motives for these duels were often mere pretexts, because they essentially consisted of tests. Still, in some cases they certainly took the form of actual duels, based on the distinctive concept of upholding the honour of the corporation, for which a rigorous code was enforced. For example, a member from one corporation was not allowed to engage in a duel with a merchant, a professional figure, or even a banker, but only with a fellow student, graduate, officer, aristocrat, or other such figure. In the eyes of the peace-loving burghers, the members of these corporations were often seen as dangerous and arrogant troublemakers.

For their part, the youth regarded themselves as a kind of elite and a seminary for a higher, more virile class within the country. Nor would it all end with university. Connections would be maintained. Belonging to one of these organisations was often the best way (aside from the possession of a degree and an education) to enter special, much sought-after careers — in the field of diplomacy, for instance. Such traditions were preserved in Germany up until the rise of Hitlerism.

Nor can it be denied that these organisations channelled energies in a unique way which, especially in Italy, are now either dissipated through sheer, disorderly, and noisy exuberance, or degraded into an infatuation with sport. Naturally, there is also the other, more recent possibility offered by politics. In previous eras, some university organisations proved themselves particularly worthy. To this day, considerable sections of the national front are constituted by zealous student organisations. Yet this is not quite the same thing, not least because the milieu and society are completely different. The structures of present-day society are often such that they no longer offer any deep existential meaning, and no outlet for one's innermost impulses. Thus, among the youth of today, and frequently among students by way of reaction or compensation, the culture of 'jocks' and 'teddy boys'[113] takes hold, not to mention even more extreme manifestations of the sort chiefly recorded on the other side of the Atlantic.

---

113 Beginning in the 1950s, a subculture emerged in the United Kingdom in which young men wore clothes in the style of Edwardian times, some of whom ending up forming violent street gangs (similar to those seen in Stanley Kubrick's film, *A Clockwork Orange*). There have been occasional attempts to revive teddy boy culture in subsequent decades. — Ed.

THE YOUTH, THE BEATS, AND RIGHT-WING ANARCHISTS

(1968)

1

Much — indeed, too much — has been written on the issue of the new generation and about 'young people'. In most cases, the topic does not deserve the interest it has received. The importance which is sometimes assigned to youth in general today, and which finds its counterpart in a sort of devaluation of all those who are not 'young', is absurd. No doubt, we are living in an age of dissolution; the increasingly prevailing condition, therefore, is that of the 'rootless' person, for whom 'society' has lost all meaning, as have the norms that used to govern life. Besides, for the age just before our own — which still endures in certain places — such norms merely coincided with those of the bourgeois world and morals. Naturally, the youth in particular have grown weary of this situation, so from this perspective it may be legitimate to address certain issues. Still, it is necessary to draw certain distinctions and consider, first of all, the case in which the situation in question is experienced in a simply passive way, and not by virtue of any active initiative of one's own, as may have been the case with the occasional intellectually-oriented, individualist rebel in the past.

A new generation, therefore, is simply accepting this state of affairs: it shows no real concern and makes foolish use of its unfettered condition, so to speak. When these young people claim that they are being misunderstood, the only answer one can give them is that there is simply nothing to understand about them — that, if a normal order were in force, it would only be a matter of curtly putting them in their place, as one does with children when their foolishness becomes annoying, invasive, and impertinent. The alleged non-conformism of some of their attitudes, which are actually quite banal, reflects a sort of trend, a new convention: it is the very opposite of an expression of freedom. Many of the phenomena we have examined in the previous pages,[114] such as the taste for vulgarity and some new social mores, may largely be attributed to this youth. Examples would include the fanatic (male and female) fans of howlers — those epileptic 'folksingers' — and, at present, of the collective puppet show known as 'yé-yé concerts'[115] and of this or that 'album', with all that such interests entail in terms of behaviour. Their lack of any sense of the ridiculous makes it impossible to exert any influence upon them, so one can only leave them to their own devices and foolishness, and consider that if any polemic with regard to things such as the sexual emancipation of minors or the sense of family should appear among this type of youth, it will be of no relevance at all. As the years go by, the need for most of them to face the material and economic problems of life will no doubt ensure that this youth, having reached adulthood, will adapt to

114 This essay is an extract from Evola's book *L'arco e la clava* (The Bow and the Club), so he is referring to the previous chapters in that book. Translation forthcoming from Arktos. — Ed.

115 'Yé-yé', inspired by the English 'yeah-yeah', was a style of Beat music that was popular throughout Western Europe in the early 1960s, exemplified by the music of Serge Gainsbourg from the time. — Ed.

the professional, productive, and social routines of the contemporary world, thereby essentially passing from one form of nothingness to another. So there is no real problem.

This type of 'youth', defined by age alone (for one can hardly speak here of certain possibilities characteristic of youth in an inner, spiritual sense),[116] is particularly common in Italy. Federal Germany[117] presents a very different phenomenon: the foolish and degenerated forms just mentioned are far less widespread there; the new generation would appear to have calmly accepted the idea of an existence in which no concerns should be raised, of a life whose meaning or purpose one should not wonder about. This generation is simply concerned with enjoying the comforts and eases offered by new development in Germany. We may refer to this type of youth as being one 'without concerns' which may have shed many conventions and acquired new freedoms, without creating any conflicts, on a two-dimensional level of 'factuality', foreign to any higher interest in myths, disciplines, or ideals.

This is probably only a transitional phase for Germany, because if we turn to consider countries that have gone further in the same direction, countries almost completely steeped in the atmosphere of a 'welfare society', where life is safe and everything is rationally regimented — we may refer in particular to Denmark, Sweden, and to some extent Norway too — we will notice that, from time to time, reactions take place in the form of violent and unexpected outbursts. These mainly concern the youth. In these cases, the phenomenon is a more interesting one and may be worth examining.

---

116 Cf. Julius Evola, 'Biological Youthfulness and Political Youthfulness', pp. 90–94 of the present volume. — Ed.

117 Meaning West Germany. — Ed.

2

In order to grasp the most typical forms of this phenomenon, it is necessary to turn to America and, to some extent, England. In America, phenomena of spiritual trauma and revolt have already emerged on a wide scale among the new generation. I am referring to that generation which has been given the name of the Beat Generation, and which I have already discussed in the previous pages: Beats or Beatniks, also known as hipsters. They have been the representatives of a sort of anarchistic and anti-social existentialism, of a more practical than intellectual sort (some insignificant literary expressions aside). At the time I am writing these lines, the movement is no longer in vogue or flourishing: it has practically disappeared from the scene or dissolved. Nonetheless, it retains a certain significance, because this phenomenon is intrinsically connected to the very nature of our twilight civilisation; so long as this civilisation endures, similar manifestations are bound to appear, albeit in different forms and under different names. In particular, as American society, more than any other, embodies the limits and the *reductio ad absurdum* of the entire contemporary system, the Beat forms of the phenomenon of revolt have acquired a special paradigmatic character; and, of course, they should not be regarded in the same terms as that foolish youth that has just been discussed, chiefly with reference to Italy.[118]

From our perspective, a brief study of certain issues within this context is justified, because I agree with the claim made by some Beats that — contrary to what psychiatrists, psychoanalysts, and 'social workers' believe — in a society and civilisation such as ours, and especially the American one, it is generally in the rebel, the misfit, and the

---

118 At the moment we are writing these lines (1968), this silly and carnivalesque Italian youth has taken to describing itself as Beat, and makes widespread use of the term. On the level of engagement, there can be no comparison between the American Beat movement, problematic as it may have been, and the ridiculous 'protest' attitude of these Italian epigones of the Beats.

anti-social person that the healthy man is to be found. In an abnormal world, all values are inverted: it is precisely the one who appears abnormal in relation to the existing milieu who is most likely to be 'normal' and to preserve some vital energy. I cannot agree at all with those who would like to 'rehabilitate' such individuals, whom they regard as sick, and to 'readapt' them to 'society'. One psychoanalyst, Robert Lindner,[119] had the courage to state this explicitly. From our point of view, the only problem concerns the definition of what we might call the 'Right-wing anarchist'. We will examine the distance that separates this type from the problematic orientation that almost invariably distinguishes the non-conformism of the Beats and hipsters.[120]

The starting point, which is to say the condition triggering the revolt of the Beats, is evident. Their target is a system that, without taking 'totalitarian' political forms, stifles life and damages personality. Sometimes the issue of physical insecurity in the future is brought up, as the very existence of mankind is seen to be threatened by the prospect of nuclear war (which are blown up to apocalyptic proportions). But what is chiefly felt is the danger of spiritual death

119 Robert M Lindner (1914–1956) was the author of the popular 1944 book, *Rebel Without a Cause: The Hypnoanalysis of a Criminal Psychopath*, which recounts numerous sessions Lindner had exploring the roots of the psychopathology of a patient named Harold. The title was later used for the famous 1955 James Dean film. — Ed.

120 In what follows we will partly be drawing upon testimonies and essays from the collected volume S. Krim (ed.), *The Beats*. The most important essays are those by H. Gold, Marc Reynold, and N. Podhoretz; to these one may add Norman Mailer's book *Advertisements for Myself*. Mailer has also been a spokesman for the Beats and hipsters, and it seems that he did not stop at mere theory, going so far as to 'gratuitously' stab his wife. As for the general climate, we may refer to Jack Kerouac's novels *On the Road* and *The Dharma Bums*, to which we may further add Colin Wilson's novel *Ritual in the Dark*, which tackles the same issues to some extent. In a book that had roused much interest, *The Outsider*, Wilson had already studied — from a general perspective — the figure of 'the outsider' (to the 'normal' world and society).

inherent in any adaptation to the current system and to its variously conditioning power ('external conditioning'). America is described as 'a rotten country, developing cancer in every one of its cells' — 'passivity (conformity), anxiety, and boredom: its three characteristics'. In such a climate, the condition of being rootless, a unit lost in the 'lonely crowd',[121] is very vividly experienced: 'society: an empty, meaningless word'. Traditional values have been lost, the new myths have been debunked, and this 'demythologisation' undermines all new hopes: 'freedom, social revolution, peace — nothing but hypocritical lies'. The prospect of 'self-alienation as the ordinary condition' is a real threat.

Here, however, one can already point to the most important difference from the 'Right-wing anarchist' type: the Beat does not react or rebel from a positive standpoint — which is to say, by having a precise idea of what a normal and sensible order would be, and firmly keeping to certain fundamental values. He reacts against the prevailing situation as though by instinct, in a confused, existential way reminiscent of certain biological reactions. By contrast, the 'Right-wing anarchist' knows what he wants; he has grounds for saying 'no'. The Beat, in his chaotic revolt, not only lacks any such grounds, but would probably reject them were they shown to him. Hence, the definition 'rebel without a flag' or 'rebel without a cause' fits him well. This implies a fundamental weakness, in that the Beats and hipsters who are so wary of being 'externally conditioned' — that is to say, controlled by external forces — ultimately run precisely this risk, insofar as their attitudes, as mere reactions, are provoked by the situation at hand. If anything, cold detachment would be a more coherent attitude.

---

121 *The Lonely Crowd* was the title of a highly influential sociological study of post-war America published in 1950. The study determined that American life was becoming less determined by things such as traditional values, institutions, but that Americans were instead beginning to live for the pursuit of material goods and were conforming to whatever they thought would help them to gain acceptance of those around them. — Ed.

Therefore, leaving aside the outwardly directed protest and revolt of the *Beat*, when this type considers the actual problem of his inner personal life and seeks to resolve it, he inevitably finds himself on slippery ground. Lacking a concrete inner centre, he throws himself into the fray, often driven by impulses which, instead of driving him forward, make him regress as he strives to fill the emptiness of a meaningless life in all possible ways. An illusory solution had been found by one of the forerunners of the Beats, Thoreau, who had resurrected the Rousseauesque myth of the natural man and of the flight into nature: an all too simplistic and, ultimately, insipid formula. Then there are those who have taken the route of a new and cruder form of bohemian living, of nomadism and vagrancy (as in the case of Kerouac's characters), of the disorder and unpredictability of an existence that shuns all pre-ordained lines of action and all discipline (as in the case of Henry Miller's early, partly autobiographical novels), in an attempt to grasp the fullness of life at every moment ('burning consciousness of the present, with neither "good" nor "evil"').[122]

The situation becomes even more serious when extreme solutions are adopted: when an attempt is made to fill one's inner emptiness, to feel 'real' and display a higher freedom ('the self under no law or obligation') through violent or even criminal actions which are conceived not just as acts of extreme resistance and protest against the established order, against what is normal and rational, but as a means to find self-confirmation. Along these lines, one has affirmed the 'moral' basis of gratuitous crimes, which is to say those carried out without any material or passionate motives, but simply out of 'a desperate need for value', to 'prove to oneself that one is a man', that 'one is not afraid of oneself', as a 'gamble with death and the afterlife'. The use of every-

---

122 A quote from Mailer's essay, 'The White Negro', which appears in his book *Advertisements for Myself* (New York: Putnam, 1959). — Ed.

thing frenetic, irrational and violent — the 'frenetic desire to create or destroy' — may be understood in much the same terms.

Here, the illusory and equivocal nature of solutions of this kind emerges quite clearly. It is evident that in such cases the search for a heightened vital feeling almost invariably serves as an illusory substitute for a real sense of the self. Besides, it is worth noting that extreme and irrational acts are not limited to things such as going out into the streets and shooting the first person one meets (as André Breton once proposed to the 'Surrealists'),[123] or raping one's younger sister, but also includes acts such as, for instance, giving away or destroying everything one owns, and risking one's life to save a foolish stranger. It is a matter of being able to discern whether what one regards as a 'gratuitous' extreme act actually attests to and realises a superior freedom, or whether it is instead driven by some hidden impulses to which one is enslaved. A serious misunderstanding on the part of anarchist individualists, generally speaking, is constituted by the idea that one is 'being oneself, free from bonds', when one is in fact enslaved to oneself. Herbert Gold's observation in regard to those cases in which this self-examination is missing is certainly correct: 'The hipster is victim of the most hopeless condition of slavery — the slave who does not know that he is a slave and is proud of his slavery, calling it "freedom"'.[124]

There is more to this. Many intense experiences that can give the Beat a fleeting sense of 'reality' ultimately make him even less 'real', as they condition him. Wilson very clearly brings this situation to light through one of the characters in his aforementioned book: someone

---

123 André Breton (1896–1966) was a French writer who was the founder of the Surrealist movement. He made this statement in 1930, in the *Second Manifesto of Surrealism*. — Ed.

124 Herbert Gold (b. 1924) is an American writer who was involved with the Beat Generation. This quote appears in his 1958 essay, 'The Beat Mystique', which was reprinted in *On Bohemia: The Code of the Self-Exiled* (London: Transaction Publishers, 1990). — Ed.

who, in a rather Beat setting, carries out a series of sadistic murders of women in order to 'become reintegrated' and escape frustration, 'as if [one had] been robbed of the powers of a god . . . as if we ought to be gods, as if the freedom of the gods ought to belong to us naturally, but something's taken it away',[125] but in the end turns out to be a shattered being, estranged from reality. 'He's like a man with paralysis who needs stronger and stronger stimulants. He doesn't care anymore.'[126] 'I thought he wanted to express revolt against the way things are nowadays. I thought [murder] was a kind of escape from personality . . . The more they talk about law and society, the more the crime rate increases . . . I thought his crimes were a gesture of defiance, like eating the apple [of Eden]. They weren't. He killed for the same reason a dipsomaniac drinks—he couldn't stop.'[127] The same also applies, of course, to any other 'extreme' experience.

In passing, in order to draw further precise distinctions, it is worth mentioning the fact that the world of Tradition was also familiar with the so-called 'Left-Hand Path'[128]—a path I have already discussed elsewhere:[129] it includes breaking the law, destruction, and the orgiastic experience in various forms, yet starting from a positive, sacred, and 'sacrificial' orientation that is directed 'upwards', towards the tran-

---

125 Colin Wilson, *Ritual in the Dark* (London: Victor Gollancz, 1959; reprinted Berkley, CA: Ronin Publishing, 1993), p. 208. — Ed.

126 Ibid., p. 410. — Ed.

127 Ibid., p. 412. — Ed.

128 In esotericism, a dichotomy is understood between the Right-Hand Path, which is identified with following a code of ethics and practicing humility, whereas practitioners of Left-Hand Path traditions often break ethical codes and violate moral and social taboos in the pursuit of enlightenment and seek to increase their personal power. In Hindu culture (as well as others), the left hand is symbolic of uncleanliness. — Ed.

129 *Eros and the Mysteries of Love* (Rochester, VT: Inner Traditions, 1993), § 28; *The Yoga of Power* (Rochester, VT: Inner Traditions, 1992), Chapter 5.

scendence of all limits. This is the opposite of the pursuit of violent sensations merely because one is internally shattered and unstable, as a means to somehow remain on one's feet. The title of Wilson's book, *Ritual in the Dark*, is most appropriate: it almost conveys the idea of celebrating in the darkness and gloom that which, in a different context, might have constituted a rite of transfiguration.

Likewise, the Beats often make use of certain drugs, seeking thereby to induce a rupture, an opening beyond ordinary consciousness. This, at any rate, is according to the intentions of the best among them. But even one of the movement's leading representatives, Norman Mailer, has acknowledged the 'gamble' which drug use entails. Alongside the 'higher clarity', the 'new, fresh, and original perception of reality, by now unknown to common man' to which some aspire by the use of drugs, there is the danger of 'artificial paradises',[130] of surrendering to forms of ecstatic delight, intense sensations, and even visions, devoid of any spiritual or revealing content, and followed by a state of depression once one returns to normality — which only aggravates the existential crisis. What makes a difference here is, once again, the fundamental attitude of one's being: this almost invariably determines the action of certain drugs, in one sense or another. Confirmation of this comes from the effects of mescaline, as described by Aldous Huxley (an author already acquainted with traditional metaphysics), who draws an analogy with certain experiences of high mysticism, as opposed to the utterly banal effects described by Zaehner[131] (an author I have already

---

130 This term was first coined by the French poet Charles Baudelaire in a book of the same name on the subject of opium and hashish, from 1860. — Ed.

131 Robert Charles Zaehner (1913–1974) was a British scholar of comparative religion and mysticism. He was a critic of the idea, central to the traditionalists as well as others, that there was a hidden metaphysical unity behind all the major religions. Zaehner held that different religious attitudes produce different types of mystical experiences in their practitioners, including those produced by drugs. — Ed.

mentioned when criticising Cuttat),[132] who sought to repeat Huxley's experiences with the aim of 'controlling' them, but starting from a completely different personal equation and attitude. Since the Beat presents himself as a profoundly traumatised being who has thrown himself into the confused pursuit of something, he cannot expect anything really positive from the use of drugs. The other alternative will almost inevitably prevail, thus reversing the initial effects.[133] Besides, the problem is not resolved by fleeting openings into 'Reality', following which one finds oneself plunged back into a meaningless life. That the prerequisites for venturing onto this ground are missing is also obvious from the fact that the vast majority of Beats and hipsters were

132 Jacques-Albert Cuttat (1909–1989) was a Swiss Frenchman who was a diplomat by profession, being the Swiss ambassador to India at one time, and he was also a friend of Frithjof Schuon. He participated in the latter's Alawiyya Order as a Muslim until he broke with Schuon in 1950, and he returned to Catholicism the following year. He continued to advocate a traditionalist perspective. Evola's essay on Cuttat, 'On the Problem of the Meeting of Religions in East and West', is available at www.counter-currents.com/2013/05/on-the-problem-of-the-meeting-of-religions-in-east-and-west/. — Ed.

133 One Beat, Jack Green, has provided (in the above-mentioned anthology) some interesting descriptions of his experiences with a particular drug, peyote. He ultimately acknowledges that this substance 'felt very nice but was no major liberation', and that if his eye had been trained, he would not have needed peyote. Moreover, regardless of what positive insights he may have reached, he shows an awareness of the *satori* doctrine of Zen. Finally, he states, 'I haven't had the true experience & I don't try for it often'. Moreover, he acknowledges the wide range of possible effects. He writes, among other things, 'it must be that the exhaustive preparation, especially the unconscious preparation involved in meditation, leads to a sudden split, which is perceived as a sudden unity'. Even after the decline of the Beat movement, American youths, and especially university students, have hardly abandoned the path of drugs. At the time of writing these lines, this is confirmed by the alarm caused by the growing spread among the youth of LSD-25 (lysergic acid diethylamide).

young people who lacked the required maturity, and who rejected all
forms of self-discipline as a matter of principle.

Some people have claimed that what the Beats (or at any rate some
of them) were seeking for, deep down, was a new religion. Mailer,
who stated 'I'm waiting for God to show me his face',[134] even claimed
that they are the harbingers of a new religion, that their excesses and
revolts are transitional forms, which 'tomorrow could give rise to a
new religion, like Christianity'. All this sounds like nonsense and today, now that it is possible to draw an assessment, no developments of
the sort are to be found. Certainly, what these forces lack are precise,
superior, and transcendent points of reference, like those of religions,
which would be capable of providing support and a right orientation.
'They are searching for a faith that will save them', someone has said,
but according to Mailer, 'God is in danger of dying'[135] — the reference
here being to the God of Western theistic religion. Thus, the so-called
mystic Beats have looked elsewhere: they have been drawn to Eastern
metaphysics, and especially Zen — as already mentioned in another
chapter. However, with regard to this last point, there are grounds for
suspicion as to the motivations involved. Zen has exerted an influence
on the individuals in question, particularly as a doctrine promising
sudden and spontaneous, enlightening openings onto Reality (with
so-called *satori*),[136] which may be produced through the undermining
and rejection of all rational superstructures through pure irrationality,
the ruthless tearing down of every idol, and possibly the use of violent
means. It is easy to see how all this might appeal to the young, rootless
Westerner who cannot put up with any discipline and leads a reckless,
rebellious life. But the truth is that Zen tacitly presupposes a previous
orientation, connected to an age-old tradition, and that harsh trials

134 This was in fact said by Jack Kerouac in a television interview on the programme
     Nightbeat in September 1957. — Ed.

135 From 'Hip, Hell, and the Navigator', in *Advertisements for Myself.* — Ed.

136 *Satori* is the Japanese Buddhist term for enlightenment. — Ed.

are not ruled out (we only need to read the biographies of certain Zen masters: Suzuki,[137] who was the first to introduce these doctrines in the West, has literally spoken of a 'baptism of fire' as preparation for *satori*). Arthur Rimbaud spoke of a method of becoming a seer through the systematic derangement of the senses,[138] and the possibility cannot be ruled out that, in a completely, mortally reckless life, in which one advances on his own, without any guidance, 'openings' of the sort alluded to by Zen may take place. But these would always be exceptions, almost miraculous occurrences — as if one were predestined, or under the protection of a good genius. One may suspect that the reason behind the attraction that Zen and similar doctrines exert on the Beats rather lies in the fact that they provide a sort of spiritual justification for their inclination towards a purely negative anarchy, towards the lack of restraint, while allowing them to avoid the primary task, which in their case would be to give oneself an inner form.

This confused need to achieve a higher, supra-rational point of reference, and — as someone has noted — to grasp 'the secret call of Being', is completely misdirected when this 'Being' is confused with 'Life', according to theories such as those of Jung and Reich.[139] This is

---

137 DT Suzuki (1870–1966) was a Japanese professor and scholar of Buddhism and Zen who wrote many books on those topics which helped to introduce them to the West. — Ed.

138 Arthur Rimbaud (1854–1891) was one of the most important French poets of the nineteenth century, classified as one of the Decadents. A prodigy, he began publishing at age 15 and quit writing forever by age 21. The technique to which Evola is referring was described by Rimbaud in a letter to Paul Demeny written on 15 May 1871. It can be found in *I Promise to Be Good: The Letters of Arthur Rimbaud* (New York: Modern Library, 2003). — Ed.

139 Wilhelm Reich (1897–1957) was an Austrian psychologist of Jewish descent who fled to the United States. He believed that sexual repression was at the root of all the ills of the modern world, including fascism. He is known for his theory of orgone energy, which he believed was the creative force in nature, and which was manifested during sex. He had a great influence on the Beat Generation. — Ed.

also the case when one sees in the sexual orgasm, and in giving oneself over to the sort of degenerate and frenzied Dionysianism sometimes offered by Negro jazz, other suitable paths for 'feeling real' and getting in touch with Reality.[140]

With regard to sex, I should repeat here what I have already stated in Chapter 12, when examining the perspectives of the apostles of the 'sexual revolution'. One of the characters in Wilson's aforementioned novel wonders whether 'the need for a woman is only the need to regain that intensity for a moment'[141] — whether a higher impulse, towards a higher freedom, is not unconsciously channelled into the sexual drive. This question is a legitimate one. As has already been noted, the non-biological and non-sensualist but, in a sense, transcendent conception of sexuality actually finds specific and significant antecedents in traditional teachings. However, it is necessary to turn here to the issue I have examined in *Eros and the Mysteries of Love*, where I have highlighted the ambivalence of the sexual experience, which is to say both the positive possibilities it encloses and the regressive, 'derealising', and conditioning ones. The starting point is a sort of existential anguish, so much so that the Beat seems to be obsessed with the idea of failing to attain 'the perfect orgasm' — according to the aforementioned views of Wilhelm Reich, and, partly, those of DH Lawrence, who claimed to see a means to merge with the primordial energy of life in sex, taken for Being and the spirit. Things being so, there are grounds for thinking that the negative and dissipating aspects of the sexual experience will predominate — once again, because the existential prerequisites for the opposite to happen are missing: sex and the uncontrollable force of the orgasm will control the self and not vice-versa, as ought to be the case in order for all of this to serve as a path. As in the case of

---

140 Casual remarks such as the following one by Mailer are typical: 'The hipster, though he respects Zen, prefers to get his mystical illumination directly from the body of a woman.' [From *Advertisements for Myself.* — Ed.]

141 *Ritual in the Dark*, p. 208. — Ed.

drugs, experiences of this sort — which, incidentally, may also play a role in the Left-Hand Path — are not suitable for an uncentred young generation. As for complete sexual freedom, as a mere expression of revolt and non-conformity, it is something trivial, which has nothing to do with the issue of spirituality. The negative aspects are brought more clearly into focus by the fact that the Beats turn jazz into a sort of religion and see it as a positive means to overcome their 'alienation', to grasp moments of liberating intensity. The Negro origins of jazz (which continue to serve as the basis of even the more elaborate forms of these rhythms, as in the case of swing and be-bop) are not seen as a matter of concern, but as something valuable. In another chapter, I have already mentioned, as an aspect of the spiritual 'negrification' of America, the fact that in a famous essay of his, Mailer assimilates the position of the Beat to that of the Negro: he speaks of the former as a 'white Negro', expressing appreciation for certain aspects of the irrational, 'natural', instinctual, and violent Negro nature. Moreover, the Beats have openly displayed a tendency towards promiscuity even on the sexual level, with White girls challenging 'prejudices' and conventions by giving themselves to Negroes. As for jazz, one can identify in its milieus an assimilation of certain elements that are more serious than the infatuation displayed by the foolish non-American youth mentioned at the beginning of this chapter. But this is precisely what makes the phenomenon more dangerous: there are reasons to believe that the identification with frenzied and elementary rhythms produces forms of 'downward self-transcendence' (to use an expression previously explained), forms of sub-personal regression to what is merely vital and primitive, partial possessions that, following moments of violent intensity and quasi-ecstatic outbursts, leave one feeling even more empty and estranged from reality than before. If we consider the atmosphere of Negro rites and group ceremonies of which jazz is reminiscent in its original and earliest forms, that direction seems quite evident: as in the case of the *macumba*[142] and in the *candomblé*[143] practised by Black Americans, it is obvious that we are dealing with forms of demonism and trance, with obscure possessions which have nothing to do with any access to a higher realm.

Unfortunately, there is little more to be gleaned from an analysis of what the Beats and hipsters have sought on an individual and existential level as a counterpart to a legitimate revolt against the present system, to fill a void and resolve the spiritual problem. The crisis situation endures. Only in exceptional cases does one find anything that, in the case of a 'Right-wing anarchist', may carry positive value. Ultimately, the matter here is one of human quality. Insofar as a new generation may choose to seriously follow the course of practical non-conformism, demythologisation and cold detachment from all bourgeois institutions, there is nothing to object. Following the suggestions of some representatives of the Beat Generation, I have not dismissed their movement as a passing trend, but have rather focused on it in some detail, on account of its distinguishing aspects. The issues it addresses are a natural expression of the current age. The movement thus preserves its significance even though its specific forms have ceased to exist in America or to exert any real appeal.

3

After all this, I would like to briefly consider a specific case related to the younger generation. There are young people who are rebelling against the sociopolitical situation in Italy while, at the same time, showing an interest in what I usually refer to as the world of Tradition.

---

142 *Macumba* is a type of magical religion practiced in parts of South America among the indigenous peoples. — Ed.

143 *Candomblé* is a highly ritualistic, orally transmitted syncretic religion practiced mainly in Brazil that developed from African religion and Islam that was brought by slaves, Catholicism, and indigenous traditions. — Ed.

While on a practical level, they oppose those Left-wing forces and ideologies which are making dangerous inroads, these youths also take an interest — at least in theory — in the teachings and disciplines of ancient lore in more positive terms than what has been the case with the Beats' confused approaches.

What we have, then, are potentially 'available' forces. The problem is that of finding the suitable guidelines to lend their activity the right direction.

My book *Ride the Tiger*, which has been described as a 'manual for the Right-wing anarchist', only partially solves this problem, since it is essentially addressed to a specific differentiated type, with a high level of maturity — something which people have failed to observe all too often. So the guidelines provided in this book are not always suitable for the category of young people I have just mentioned.

The first advice to give these youths is to be wary of forms of interest and enthusiasm that might only be biologically conditioned, which is to say connected to age. One must see whether these young people will preserve the same outlook once they approach adulthood and come to face the concrete problems of life. Unfortunately, experience has shown me that this is only rarely the case. At the threshold of thirty, say, few keep their position.

I have spoken of a kind of youth which is not merely biological, but also has an inner, spiritual aspect, and hence is not conditioned by age. This higher youth may also manifest itself through biological youth. What it is characterised by is not 'idealism' — an inflated, equivocal term — since the capacity to undermine ideals to the point of approaching point zero of established values is a trait which these young people ought to share in common with other currents, of a very different nature. I would rather speak of a certain capacity for enthusiasm and vigour, unconditional devotion, and detachment form bourgeois life and purely material and self-serving interests. The task, then, would be to assimilate these inclinations and make them one's own, so that they may become permanent qualities and counter the opposite influences to which one becomes fatally exposed with the passing of the years, and the need to face the concrete problems of contemporary life.[144] As for non-conformism, the first prerequisite is a strictly anti-bourgeois conduct of life. In his early days, Ernst Jünger did not hesitate to write that 'it was infinitely more worthwhile to be a criminal than a bourgeois.'[145] I am not saying that this formula should be taken literally, but it suggests a general orientation. In everyday life, moreover, one must look out for the snares of sentimental matters — marriage, the family, and any other surviving structure belonging to a society whose absurdity one acknowledges. This is a crucial benchmark. By contrast, in the case of the type in question, certain experiences which we have seen to be problematic in the case of Beats and hipsters may not pose the same dangers.

As a counterpart to all this, the type in question ought to display an inclination towards self-discipline in free forms, removed from any social or 'pedagogical' requirement. In the case of young people, what is at stake is their development, in the most objective sense of the term.

---

144 In this respect, it may be interesting to provide a reference drawn from the ancient Arab-Persian civilisation. The term *futâva*, from *fatà* = 'young man', was used to describe the quality of 'being young' precisely in the spiritual sense just noted, one not defined on the basis of age but primarily of a special disposition of the spirit. Thus, the *fityân* or *fityûh* (= 'the young') came to be conceived as an Order, whose members would undergo a rite connected to a kind of solemn vow always to maintain this quality of 'being young'.

145 This quote appears in Ernst Jünger's 1932 book, *The Worker*. The specific context he is referring to was the situation of German youth during the period of Germany's collapse after the First World War. The entire passage reads: 'Here the youth of Germany saw the bourgeois in his last, naked appearance, and here it pledged, in its finest incarnations, soldier and worker alike, to join at once in a rebellion which expressed clearly that, in this space, it was infinitely more worthwhile to be a criminal than a bourgeois.' (From an unpublished translation of *The Worker* that was edited and translated by Bogdan Costea and Laurence P Hemming.)

A difficulty emerges because every development entails certain values as a point of reference, but the young man in revolt rejects all values, all the 'morals' of existing society — and especially bourgeois society.

A distinction must be drawn in this respect. There are certain values which have a conformist character and a purely exterior, social justification — not to mention those values which have come to be regarded as such because their original foundations have been completely lost. Other values instead simply present themselves as a means to ensure a genuine form and steadfastness. Courage, loyalty, lack of deviousness, an aversion to falsehood, an incapacity to betray, and superiority vis-à-vis any selfish pettiness or lowly interest may be counted among those values which, in a way, transcend 'good' and 'evil', as they are situated on an ontological rather than a 'moral' level: precisely because they bestow or strengthen 'being', in contrast to the condition represented by a feeble, elusive, and shapeless nature. No 'imperative' applies here. The individual's natural disposition is what counts. To use a simile, nature presents substances which are both fully crystallised as well as those which are imperfect and incomplete crystals, mixed with crumbly gangue. Certainly, we will not call the former 'good' and the latter 'bad' in a moral sense. It is a matter of different degrees of 'reality'. The same holds true for human beings. The problem of young people's development and of their love for self-discipline must be approached on this level, above all criteria and values related to social morality. F. Thiess[146] has justly written, 'There are vulgarity, meanness, baseness, bestiality, and perfidy, just as there is the stupid practice of virtue, bigotry, and conformist respect for the law. The former are worth as little as the latter.'

Generally speaking, young people are characterised by an overflow of energy. Thus the problem emerges of what use this can be put to in a world such as ours. In this respect, one may first of all consider the

---

146 Frank Thiess (1890–1977) was a German novelist. — Ed.

fostering of the process of 'development' on the physical level. Here I can hardly recommend any modern sport at all. Indeed, sport is one of the leading causes of the degradation of the modern masses, and almost inevitably has a vulgar character. However, some particular physical activities may be acceptable. One example is high-altitude mountaineering, when it is brought back to its original form, without the technical aids and the tendency towards sheer acrobatics that have deformed it and stripped it of its spirit in recent times. Parachuting, too, can offer positive possibilities — in this case, as much as in the previous one, the risk factor is a useful support for inner strengthening. Another example might be Japanese martial arts, provided that there is an opportunity to learn them according to their original tradition and not in the forms which have become widespread in the West, which lack the spiritual counterpart that enabled these activities to be closely associated with subtle forms of inner and spiritual discipline. In relatively recent times, various possibilities were offered by certain student corporations in Central Europe, the so-called *Korpsstudenten* practising *Mensur* — cruel but non-fatal duels that followed specific rules (leaving facial scars as traces) — with the goal of developing courage, steadfastness, intrepidity, and endurance to physical pain, while at the same time upholding the values of a higher ethics, of honour and camaraderie, although not without certain excesses. But as the corresponding sociocultural contexts have disappeared, something of this sort is quite unthinkable today, especially in Italy.

This overflow of energy may also lead to various forms of 'activism' in the sociopolitical sphere. In these cases, what is required first of all is serious self-examination, to ascertain that a possible engagement with ideas opposed to the general climate may not simply be a means to release such energy (in which case, under different circumstances, even very different ideas might serve the same purpose). The starting point and driving force must rather be a true identification with these ideas, based on a thoughtful acknowledgement of their intrinsic value.

A part from this, in the case of activism a further difficulty emerges: for although the type of youth I have been referring to may have clearly discerned which ideas are worth fighting for, he could hardly find any fronts, parties, or political groups which truly and staunchly defend ideas of that sort in the current climate. Another circumstance, namely the fact that the stage we have reached makes it unlikely for the struggle against the presently dominant political and social movements to achieve any appreciable general results, ultimately has little weight: the norm here should be to do what must be done, while being ready to fight — if necessary, even a losing battle. At any rate, affirming a certain 'presence' today even by means of action will always be useful.

As for the sort of anarchist activism that constitutes a mere act of protest, this could range from the kind of violent demonstrations that are commonly described as 'hooliganism' — such as those held by young people in certain countries (I have already mentioned the case of Northern European countries, where 'welfare society' is the rule) — to terrorist acts, such as those once used by the nihilist political anarchists. Leaving aside the motives of certain Beats, which is to say the desire to carry out violent actions simply for the thrill they give, such activism seems quite pointless even simply as a means to release some energy. Certainly, if it were possible to set up a sort of 'Holy Vehme'[147] today, so as to keep the main culprits of contemporary subversion in a constant state of physical insecurity, it would be an excellent thing. But this is not something which the youth can organise; and, besides, the defence system of contemporary society is too well-built for such initiatives not to be quashed from the start and paid for at too high of a price.

It is worth considering one last point. In the category of young people that we are presently discussing, and who may be described as

---

147 The Holy Vehme were vigilante courts, which often met in secret, in the Westphalia region of Germany during the Middle Ages, sanctioned by the Holy Roman Emperor and empowered to carry out death sentences. — Ed.

Right-wing anarchists in relation to the contemporary milieu, we find some individuals who are seriously drawn at the same time towards the prospects for spiritual realisation that have been brought to their attention by earnest representatives of the traditionalist movement,[148] with reference to ancient lore and initiatory doctrines. This is something more serious than the aforementioned ambiguous interest exerted by the irrationalism of a misunderstood Zen among some American Beats, not least because of the different quality of the sources of information. Such an attraction is understandable, considering the spiritual vacuum that has been created by the decadence of the religious forms once dominant in the West and the questioning of their value. It is not inconceivable that, once removed from these, young people may aspire towards something truly superior, rather than any worthless substitutes. Nonetheless, with regard to the youth our aspirations must not be too ambitious and removed from reality. Not only is a certain degree of maturity required, but one must also bear in mind that the path which I have also outlined in previous chapters (11 and 15) requires, and has always required, special qualifications and something akin to what is known as a 'vocation' among religious Orders. As is well known, in such Orders the novice is allowed a certain amount of time to ascertain just how genuine his vocation is. Here I must repeat what I have stated before concerning the more general vocation that one may experience as a youth: it is necessary to see whether it will grow weaker or stronger with the passing years.

The doctrines to which I have referred must not give rise to the kind of illusions upheld by many spurious forms of contemporary neo-spiritualism — Theosophy, Anthroposophy, and so on — which is

---

148 Traditionalism refers to the school of religious thought which follows in the tradition of René Guénon, and includes Evola himself, although Guénon himself rejected the idea of 'traditionalism', as he believed that his teachings were only explicating what was already present in the doctrines of the traditional religions, rather than presenting something innovative. — Ed.

to say, to the idea that the highest goal is within everyone's reach and realisable by this or that expedient. Rather, it should appear as a distant peak, to be reached only through a long, difficult, and dangerous trek. Certain preliminary tasks of considerable import are nonetheless a real prospect for those nurturing a genuine interest. First of all, they should devote themselves to a series of studies concerning the general view of life and of the world which constitutes the natural counterpart to such doctrines so as to acquire a new outlook, positively reinforcing the 'no' they utter to all that exists today, and to eliminate the many and severe forms of intoxication that are a result of modern culture. The second phase, the second task, would be to surpass the merely intellectual level by lending 'organic' form to a certain set of ideas in such a way that it may determine a fundamental existential orientation, and thereby engender a permanent and unwavering sense of security. Any youths who had gradually attained as much would have already gone a very long way. They could leave open the question of the 'if' and 'when' of the *third* phase, in which, with the enduring of the original tension, one may attempt certain actions that are 'deconditioning' with respect to human limits. Imponderable factors come into play here, and the only sensible aim to pursue is an adequate preparation. It would be absurd to expect any immediate results in a youth.

Various personal experiences of mine confirm the relevance of these final brief considerations and clarifications, which obviously concern a highly differentiated group within the non-conformist youth: the group of those who have come to perceive the strictly spiritual problem within its appropriate framework.

These considerations have brought us well beyond what is commonly called the problem of young people. The 'Right-wing anarchist' may be conceived as a fairly distinct and comprehensible type, in opposition to both the stupefied youth and the 'rebels without a flag', and to all those who embrace reckless living and undertake experiences that can provide no real solution, no positive contribution, unless one already possesses an inner form. Strictly speaking, one could object that this form is a limitation, a bond which contradicts the initial aspiration, the absolute freedom of anarchism. However, it is highly unlikely that anyone formulating such an objection may do so by taking as his point of reference transcendence in the genuine and absolute sense of the term — the kind of sense, for example, it acquires in relation to high ascesis. Hence, one may reply that the other alternative concerns a youth that is so 'burned out' that, as no significant core has survived the test represented by the general dissolution, it may well be regarded as a pure existential product of this very same dissolution: it is pure delusion for this youth to believe that it is really free. Such a youth, whether rebellious or not, is of very little interest to us — nor do we have anything to do with it. It can only serve as a case study within the overall framework of the pathology of an epoch.

SOME OBSERVATIONS ON THE STUDENT MOVEMENT

(1968)

Much has been written about the student unrest — too much, in our view. We wondered whether it was worth our while to make some observations concerning the topic ourselves. Given that certain representatives of the student movement had seen it fit to exchange views with us, we sought to discover first-hand what aims this movements had set itself, at least in Italy. We must confess that our findings proved something of a disappointment.

Naturally, what we were potentially interested in were chiefly the reasons behind those protests that were not confined to technical university problems. It is evident that the demands advanced with regard to such problems, the charges levelled against an obsolete and poorly-functioning university, have often been merely a pretext. These problems could have been solved in their suitable, administrative context without causing such an uproar and with no particular ideological implications. Exerting some pressure through direct action in order to reach reasonable solutions would also have been plausible, given the bureaucratic inertia. But things did not stop there. As an overview of the protests across different countries reveals, the aforementioned problems have only been a pretext or starting point.

By turning a well-known saying around, one might say that the agitators of the student movements sought to bring forth a mountain from a mouse when, having gained momentum, they chose to carry out an attack against the current system as a whole. Their favourite target is the so-called civilisation of consumption in the technologically advanced societies of the bourgeois world. Just to what degree this extension of the 'protest' has been manipulated by Left-wing elements is well-known, yet it is equally indisputable that the attitude displayed by the two is much the same. Even in the case of the Italian student movement, varied as it may be, certain claims that have been advanced and catchwords which have been coined for the reform of the university system have a revealing character. Indeed, it is one thing to denounce the 'homogenisation' of the university system, inadequacies in terms of resources or even teaching, and certain biases in the choice of subjects; it is quite another to invoke ridiculous formulas, such as the 'democratisation' of universities, and to indict the current system as an intolerably authoritarian 'bosses' school' or 'classist' one (as though all students were proletarians). The spirit behind these attitudes and the defiance it fuels is clear, and constitutes a far from positive indicator regarding the orientation of the student movement.

Strictly speaking, given that the current political system in Italy is the democratic one, with the aforementioned extension of the 'protest', the catchword ought to have been anti-democracy, first of all. Instead, as already noted, what is being deplored is the fact that the university system itself is not 'democratic' enough. This defiance of the principle of authority is not based on a few individual cases of despicable behaviour on the part of the teaching staff (besides, the dominant orientation among our lecturers is Marxism); rather, it is directed towards the structures and authorities themselves. It is natural, therefore, that in Communist countries, where the dominant form of authority is the Communist one, the student protest often acquires an anti-Communist veneer. No positive inference is to be drawn from all this precisely because defiance is shown towards authority in general, regardless of the forms it may take — to the point that, for instance, the most trite anti-fascist pretexts find fertile soil, and some people would go as far as to speak of an unbearably 'fascist' type of school and teaching.

But if there was ever a field in which the existence of a principle of authority seems natural, legitimate, and unquestionable, it is precisely in the field of learning. Those who do not know must acknowledge the authority of those who do — of those who possess knowledge and suitable means to convey it, based on long experience and an established tradition. There is nothing humiliating in this.

It is only natural to ask for the teaching imparted to be further clarified or integrated. So-called university 'seminars', which are especially common abroad, have already introduced forms of cooperation and proximity between teachers and eager students, without the slightest subversive or 'revolutionary' note.

A very different situation emerges when we turn to examine the claims of the anti-authoritarian students in detail. We will find that what is ultimately being pursued is a sort of school soviet, the establishment of what is known as the 'collective' in the Communist system. With this, the mask falls away. It also falls when, instead of asking for the university system to be progressively de-politicised and brought back to a serious system of study with no ideological interferences, the very opposite goal is pursued. Have some people not deplored the fact that lecturers do not officially discuss Vietnam, Mao, and other newfangled political topics with their students? The spirit according to which these discussions are meant to take place is all too clear. In any case, political topics of some contemporary relevance should, at most, only be considered as a side note in political science departments. A serious student cannot require political intrusions of this sort as far as the vast majority of other disciplines are concerned — the natural sciences, medicine, engineering, chemistry, and so on. Students can vent their views as much as they want outside the university. In our view, safeguarding the non-political character of a serious system of study is a crucial requirement. If anything, a revolt should take the opposite direction, meaning that it should be directed against the harmful ideological pressure and influences that, in the present context within the Marxist or 'democratic-Marxist'[149] climate, are exerted wherever possible — for instance, in the field of the teaching of history, sociology, literature, and philosophy.

But let us now return to the superordinate claim of the student movement, which is seriously taken into consideration by those seeking to 'idealise' the youth, namely: the claim that starting from the university world, the all-out protest should be extended and directed against the 'system' as a whole, against the contemporary form of society and civilisation. At best, one might assume that what lies in the background here is a feeling of spiritual emptiness, a sense of the lack of any profound meaning to modern life. Thus, Marcuse[150] has often unwittingly served as the philosopher of the movement.

We have noted the spiritually destructive character of what Marcuse presents as the distinctive features of technologically advanced societies and of the civilisation of consumption. Given this background,

---

149 In Italian, *demomarxista*. The Italian Fascists often spoke of *demoplutocratico*, merging the Greek *demos* (people) with plutocracy — it is likely that Evola is coining a similar term. — Ed.

150 Herbert Marcuse (1898–1979) was a German Marxist intellectual who was part of the Frankfurt School. In 1964 he published his most influential work, *One Dimensional Man*, which was a critique of both capitalism and Soviet-style Communism. In it, he argued that advanced industrial civilisations reduce individuals to consumers, conditioning them into desiring false needs through mass media and propaganda. He believed that the only path to true freedom lay in an individual's 'great refusal' of the ideas and products of present-day society. His ideas became very influential in the international New Left of the 1960s and '70s. The then-leader of the MSI, Giorgio Almirante, once famously remarked that Evola was 'our Marcuse — only better.' — Ed.

two points are worth emphasising. First of all, there is an absolute lack of positive points of reference, of values on the basis of which a different system might be set up as a counterpart to the present one. (In this regard, Marcuse makes no concrete suggestions at all; one of his merits, in our view, is to have ruled out Marxism and Communism as possible points of reference through the suggestion that, by increasingly fulfilling the rather bourgeois needs and aspirations of the working class, the technological civilisation of consumption and well-being absorbs this class, thereby putting an end to its 'protest'). Secondly, it is worth noting the nature of the aforementioned claim: how could a protest movement, starting from the universities, undermine the whole system, since what is at stake here is no longer ideologies or superstructures but infrastructures determined by science and technology in a world of masses and production?

To start with a small observation, in order to be consistent, the 'all-out' protest of the youth should follow a completely different direction: instead of screaming for reform, they should simply stop going to university. For what is the ultimate purpose of attending universities and similar educational institutes after the completion of a more general course of study? In the case of most departments, it is to pursue a kind of training and specialisation in order to obtain an academic title that will enable one to find a place — where? Precisely in the abhorred technological consumer society, thereby furnishing it with fresh recruits. To take things even further, destructive anarchism would be the only remaining option: to blow up or set fire to the police headquarters, manufacturing plants, technological institutes, and so on — with a 'student power' movement emulating the gestures of 'Black Power' on a wider scale. To tell the truth, forms of destructive frenzy, vandalism, and senseless destruction have already emerged here and there in the recent student upheavals. These are indicative of one of the darkest driving forces behind such events. Yet no one can seriously consider the possibility of this anarchism reaching apocalyptic proportions. An effective general uprising against a whole organised world accepted by the masses is a sheer chimaera, given that the vast majority of people would in no way be ready to renounce the comforts of the 'civilisation of consumption' and 'well-being' — however standardised and conditioning this may be — in the name of an abstract idea of freedom.

'Protests' concerning 'cultural freedom' may fit into a more reasonable framework. The right course of action would be to reappraise university studies in such a way as to restrict technological specialisation and bring back to the fore the 'humanistic' education of young people through a range of disciplines of limited practical value but intrinsic worth — particularly as a means of bestowing a higher meaning on life, of shaping a new worldview, and of promoting a strict conduct of living and the crystallisation of an earnest inward essence rich in meaning and character. Obviously, this approach is not be confused with what is left of the humanities in universities. The few students who continue to attend humanities departments are aiming for something that is not all that different from what the students in other departments are after: essentially, they have set their sights on what they need in order to 'find a place for themselves' by becoming part of the 'system' as teachers or through other bourgeois professions, inevitably conditioned by the present circumstances. But it is rather through the pre-eminence of a 'free culture', in the true sense of the term just mentioned, that a gradual transformation of the 'system' might possibly be brought about by the new generations, from within and without any apocalyptic utopia.

Regrettably, we have hardly ever witnessed aspirations and claims of this sort on the part of the representatives of the student movement. Apparently it is easier for them to abandon themselves to shows of vague defiance. On account of its nature, namely the lack of positive points of reference, this defiance can all too easily be exploited — as we have seen — by the forces on the Left, which actually know all too well what they want. Speaking of intellectual confusion, it is telling that what was adopted as a banner in Germany was the grotesque and rather hybrid formula of the three Ms: Marx, Mao, Marcuse. Here we would like to repeat a point already made: if the idea is to carry the movement outside the universities, which is to say outside the sphere of specific problems that can be addressed without particular ideological implications and without any drama, then the aims should not be set too high. An important preliminary task, requiring a certain degree of courage and inner freedom, would be to fight against the principle expressions of the 'system' in the contemporary sociopolitical field, namely democracy and Marxism. Only then could one acknowledge the presence of a healthy instinct in the youth, of a revolutionary impulse in the positive sense. Unfortunately, we have already noted more than one symptom which makes it difficult to reach any such conclusion.

PSYCHOANALYSIS OF THE PROTEST

(1970)

One of the signs of the breakdown of contemporary culture is the attention paid to the so-called protest movement, both in general and in its particular form as a 'youth movement'. This is not to say that the movement in question is of no importance, on the contrary; but is only of factual importance, as a token of the times, and it is exclusively in these terms that it ought to be considered.

A violent reaction against the negative aspects of the contemporary world constitutes the 'mask' of the currents in question. However, what better defines them is the fact that they consist of disorderly and anarchical instinctual reactions which are in no way justified by that in the name of which this rejection and protest is taking place. Even when no subjection to Marxist or Communist influences is apparent, the 'existential' background of this youth protest is highly questionable. One of its well-known spokesmen, Cohn-Bendit,[151] claimed that what the protesters are

---

151 Daniel Cohn-Benit (b. 1945) is a German-French Jewish politician. He was one of the student leaders of the Paris revolt in May 1968, where he was a sociology student at the University of Paris at the time. His participation brought him fame. In the 1970s he published books describing sexual encounters with children during his time as a teacher. He later became a leader in the German Green Party. He became deputy mayor of Frankfurt in 1989, where he was put in charge of multicultural matters for immigrants, and was elected to the European Parliament in 1994 for the German Greens. In 1999 he reentered the European Parliament as the leader of the French Green Party's faction, where he called for looser immigration restrictions. He is currently the Co-President of the European Greens–European Free Alliance. — Ed.

fighting for is a 'new man'; but he forgot to say what kind of man this might be. And should the vast majority of present-day protesters serve as a model for this 'new man' in terms of their individuality, behaviour, and choices, then one could only reply: thanks, but we'd rather do without it. Given the lack of any genuinely positive counterpart and the predominance of an irrational substrate, it would be fair to say that the protest movement requires not so much a cultural analysis as an existential-psychoanalytical one. This seemed to be provided by a recently-published volume entitled *Psicodinamica della contestazione*.[152] The author, M Moreno, is a scholar in the aforementioned field of modern psychological research. Reading this work, however, one soon realises that such research ultimately lacks the principles required in order to reach any serious and plausible conclusion.

As the defining features of contemporary forms of protest, Moreno's study invokes anti-authoritarianism, and hence the defence of instinctiveness against all forms of 'repression' (especially in the sexual field), followed by an anarchical orientation. In doing so, it does not go beyond the most obvious and ostentatious aspects, without touching upon the deep and unconscious impulses which constitute the domain of psychoanalysis. This domain is only approached when, after having defined the kind of system that is being opposed as 'patriarchal' (with reference to the exercise of authority this entails), the famous Oedipus complex is brought into play. As is widely known, Freudian psychoanalysis dogmatically assumes that, within the context of a murky ancestral heritage revived by certain alleged childhood experiences, each of us suffers from this complex, which entails a revolt against one's father verging on a desire to suppress him. The collective outburst of this latent complex would thus be one of the underground roots of the contemporary protest.

---

152 Mario Moreno, *Psychodynamics of the Protest* (Torino: ERI, 1969). No English version exists. — Ed.

The argument is hardly convincing. First of all, one would have to prove that the present 'system' revolves around the ideal of the 'father' and of his authority. At most this might have been the case in Europe before the First World War. But the contemporary world is governed by democracy, socialism, egalitarianism, socialitarianism, and so on.: sociopolitical forms that go in an opposite direction, since — as others have rightly noted — they all possess a 'feminine' and 'maternal' character. What has a masculine and 'paternal' character, by contrast, is the idea of a monarchical, aristocratic, and hierarchical state, few traces of which survive nowadays. But in order to refute and at the same time elucidate the Oedipean thesis, one may first of all turn to psychoanalysis itself, which acknowledges the 'ambiguity' of the Oedipus complex: the person suffering from it does not simply hate his father, but also admires and envies him; he wishes to do away with his father simply in order to take his place and enjoy the same privileges as him.

The underlying feature of the 'protest' is precisely the fact that this last aspect is missing. The 'father' is not at all admired or 'envied'. No one wishes to take his place. The new generation sees red upon the sight of any form of authority. This brings out the other aforementioned characteristic of the protest: its purely, hysterically anarchical aspect — everything else merely serving as a pretext for it.

From a human point of view in general, this bears witness to a regressive phenomenon. People should make up their minds about the much-deplored issue of 'repression' once and for all. Plato argued that those who lack a sovereign principle within ought to at least have one without. Thus, any normal order entails certain limits which are designed less to bind than to support those who are incapable of giving themselves any law, form, and discipline. Of course, a system may enter into crisis and fossilise: in that case, the limits in question may take a stubborn and merely 'repressive' form, in an attempt to stem the disorder and dissolution. In order to turn to 'protest', however, in this case one ought to acquire legitimacy, in other words to show that it is not simply a matter of aversion towards all forms of inner discipline, but rather of yearning for a more genuine life. Yet nothing of the sort is to be observed nowadays.

What we observe, instead, are individuals identifying with the instinctive, irrational, and amorphous part of man (his 'underground') — that part which in every higher human being is not stubbornly 'repressed', but rather held at a certain distance and in check. The links between the protest movement and the most spurious and promiscuous aspects of the so-called sexual revolution, just like the fact that it is in cahoots with 'hippie' junkies and other such types, are certainly revealing, as is the spectacle offered by the many sectors in which the repressive 'system' is increasingly being replaced by a 'permissive' one.

What use is being made of this new space, this new freedom? Here the symptoms multiply, showing that the 'revolt' as a whole is influenced from below. It is the very opposite of that essentially aristocratic form of revolt that still distinguished some individualists of the previous generation, starting with Nietzsche — the best Nietzsche. It is worth quoting a few lines here from this author (who is never quoted by today's protesters, who at most are hung up on writers like Marcuse, as they instinctively perceive the different nature, the aristocratic character, of Nietzsche's far broader revolt). Zarathustra states:

> You call yourself free? Your dominating thought I want to hear, and not that you escaped from a yoke.
>
> Are you the kind of person who had the *right* to escape from a yoke? There are some who threw away their last value when they threw away their servitude.
>
> Free from what? What does Zarathustra care! But brightly your eyes should signal to me: free *for what*?[153]

---

153 Friedrich Nietzsche, *Thus Spoke Zarathustra* (Cambridge: Cambridge University Press, 2006), p. 46. — Ed.

Zarathustra warns us that being free, enjoying an amorphous personal freedom, can amount to doom and catastrophe.

Therefore, the driving force and 'psychodynamics' of the protest movement would appear to lie in that dark zone, that elementary sub-personal and sub-intellectual substrate of the human being which is the focus of psychoanalysis. What we have is the regressive and explosive emergence of these layers, in parallel to the manifold fracturing of a world in crisis. Acknowledging the questionable and deplorable aspects of this world makes no difference. When a revolutionary movement lacks the values required for a genuine restoration and is not led by a human type that embodies a higher legitimacy, all we can expect from it is a transition to an even more critical and destructive stage than the one which existed at the start.

As the present remarks have been inspired by Moreno's slim volume, in moving towards a conclusion we should like to note that, after having presented the purely Freudian, Oedipean interpretation of the unconscious substrate of the protest, this professor of psychiatry partly criticises and rejects it. Moreno rather believes that one should draw upon a theory formulated by CG Jung. As is widely known, Jung holds rather different ideas from Freud. Borrowing Plato's concept of the 'archetype' and of the metaphysical plane, Jung has transposed them to the level of the so-called 'collective unconscious'. According to this view, typical dynamic structures, the 'archetypes', lie dormant in the collective unconscious, deep within all individuals, and can resurface in critical individual or collective conditions, carrying people away. Several of these archetypes are said to exist, which are also connected to certain symbolic 'figures'. One of them is the *puer aeternus*,[154] an embodiment of the pre-conscious and native aspect of the collective soul which, like a young boy, is 'the future in potency' — and hence a principle of renewal, the restoration of all that an individual or culture has rejected or repressed in terms of vital naturalness.

---

154 Latin: 'eternal boy'. — Ed.

According to Moreno, in the light of psychoanalysis the protest movement may be seen to reflect an uncontrollable re-emergence of this archetype, the *puer aeternus*, within the new generation, which no longer identifies with the outdated symbols imposed by the 'system'. All in all, then, Moreno's verdict is a positive one.

In order to follow Moreno in his overstretched interpretation, we should start by taking Jung's 'mythology' seriously. In fact, we reject it as much as Freud's, for well-founded reasons which we have expounded elsewhere.[155] Ultimately, this quirk of the *puer aeternus* seems to be in line with the fetishisation of youth, or 'youthism', another regressive contemporary phenomenon: the idea of clearing the way for young people — regarded as the voice of the future and the harbingers of new genuine values — and of learning from them, instead of educating and training them. This fetishisation, extended even to children, had already emerged, along with anti-authoritarian considerations, with the pedagogy of Montessori[156] and other pedagogues; it was then further developed with the discovery of the child as 'creator', 'artist', and so on. With Jung, the *puer* acquired the rank of an archetype and, as we have seen in Moreno's interpretation, of a positive revolutionary archetype. Freud's essentially amusing picture of the infant as 'polymorphously perverse'[157] has therefore been overturned. On our part, we are willing

---

155 Evola attacked psychoanalysis at length in Maschera e volto dello spiritualismo contemporaneo (Mask and Face of Contemporary Spiritualism, Turin: Bocca, 1932). No English version exists. Evola essentially rejected it for overprivileging the subconscious, and for reducing mythological and religious figures to nothing more than psychological 'symbols' representing psychic processes. — Ed.

156 Maria Montessori (1870–1952) was an Italian doctor who developed an educational philosophy for young children predicated on the idea that they are better capable of teaching themselves, free from the guidance or discipline of an authority figure, and believed that this was a better method of raising children than traditional methods. — Ed.

157 Freud theorised that children from birth to the age of five can derive sexual gratification through means different from those normally accepted by society, progressing from an oral stage, and then to the anal and phallic stages. — Ed.

to accept the idea of the *puer aeternus* at work in the subconscious of the protesters (according to Moreno's perspective), but only if we take the child as a child, demythologising him — and hence with reference to an extremely annoying form of primitivism or childishness. It would be high time, then, to send this *puer* (*aeternus* or not) to bed, no matter how virulent or overbearing he may be — were it not that we live in a defeatist world.

AGAINST THE YOUNG

(1967)

One of the signs of the breakdown of contemporary Italian society is the myth of young people, the importance assigned to the problem of youth, combined with a sort of tacit devaluation of those who 'are not young'.[158] It seems as though educators and sociologists nowadays are afraid of losing touch with 'the young', without realising that in doing so they are slipping into a form of childishness. It is said that youths have something to teach us, that they can show us new paths to follow (even Christian Democrat MPs have spoken in such terms), whereas those who, because of their age, have really experienced life should step aside — the very opposite of what has always been the belief, even among primitive peoples. And we have witnessed television complacently welcoming the demonstrations and protests of these so-called young people, even when verging on the absurd or grotesque. For instance, we have heard some of them deplore the fact that schools are not 'democratic' yet, and call for something along the lines of soviets or 'internal commissions', probably with the aim of 'educating' teachers and setting them on the right track. The fact that students are occupying universities — as workers are doing with factories — for the sake of this or that 'demand', and that they are allowed to do so, or are even

---

158 Passages of this essay are repeated from a previous essay in this volume, 'The Youth, the Beats, and Right-Wing Anarchists'. — Ed.

offered protection by the police — well, it is very much in the style of 'liberated Italy'.

We are certainly living in an age of dissolution, and the condition which is becoming increasingly dominant is that of the 'rootless' individual. As 'society' no longer has any meaning for such a person, neither do the constraints formerly governing existence: constraints which in the previous age were no doubt only those of the bourgeois world and of bourgeois morality — and which in various places still endure. So it was only natural and legitimate for some problems to emerge for the youth. But the overall situation must be taken into account; every good solution should affect the whole system — everything else, including what concerns the youth, being nothing but a consequence.

The possibility that some positive suggestions may come from the vast majority of 'young people' in today's Italy is definitely to be ruled out. When these people claim that they are misunderstood, the only answer they deserve is that there is nothing to be understood from them: if a normal order existed, it would only be a matter of curtly putting them in their place, as one might do with children, when their foolishness becomes annoying, intrusive, or impertinent. Just what their non-conformism, 'protest', or 'revolt' amounts to is all too clear. It has nothing to do with the sporadic anarchists of a few decades ago, who at least were capable of thinking, and were familiar with the likes of Nietzsche and Stirner;[159] or with those who, in terms of art or worldview, enthusiastically embraced Futurism, Dadaism, or the *Sturm und*

---

159 Max Stirner (1806–1856) was a German philosopher who denied that there was such a thing as absolute truth, and who favoured the freedom of the individual through a complete liberation from all the abstract (and therefore false) concepts upon which society, in his view, is based. Although he never applied such labels to himself, Stirner is usually seen as an anarchist and nihilist. His primary work is *The Ego and Its Own*. — Ed.

Drang[160] promoted by the early Papini.[161] The 'rebels' of today are 'long-hairs' and Beats whose non-conformism is of the cheapest kind, and no matter how banal it may be, it follows a trend, a new norm. It does so in a passive, provincial way, since the Beatnik or hipster movement is already a thing of the past in America. Besides, it had produced a few literary echoes, and had taken some dangerous, destructive turns; but this is hardly the case in Italy, where intellectual deficiency and illiteracy are paramount.

Thus, among the representatives of this 'youth' one finds, among both the sexes, fanatical fans of those epileptic screamers known as 'folksingers', of the collective puppet show of 'Yé-yé concerts' and 'shake', of this or that 'album'. Look at their faces: you will hardly find one which is not vapid and does not bear the mark of a particular 'character' — starting with their idols: take the two male singers and the female one who at the moment most cause the Italian Beats to swoon (incidentally, it should be noted that 95 per cent of them ignore the actual meaning of the term 'Beat' in America). As regards ideological 'revolt', we hear these 'young people' singing that they wish to 'fight war with their guitars', for instance. They are enthusiastic about the slogan 'make love, not war', which was apparently coined by that most mediocre pacifist philosopher, Bertrand Russell. Well, then: if this were a serious revolt (even one 'without a flag', without any positive points of reference to offer as a counterpart); if, as among American hipsters,

160 'Storm and stress' is a term originally applied to an eighteenth-century German movement in drama which insisted upon the primacy of the individual and of emotions beyond the limits of Enlightenment rationalism. — Ed.

161 Giovanni Papini (1881–1956) was an Italian poet and writer who was known as a Modernist literary figure, and who also made a name for himself as a prominent atheist. He caused a great scandal by suggesting that Jesus had been in a homosexual relationship with John the Apostle. After the First World War, Papini actually returned to Catholicism, and became a prominent Fascist intellectual. — Ed.

contemporary civilisation were truly regarded as 'rotten and senseless', and consisting of 'boredom, putrid well-being, conformism, and lies'; with no apparent way out for the moment, should these 'rebels' not rather adopt as their slogan good old Marinetti's[162] formula, 'War, the world's only hygiene'[163] and carry placards reading 'Long live atomic warfare!', so as to finally make a clean slate?

It is claimed that during the flooding in Tuscany, the 'longhairs' did their best' — a sign, for some people, that ultimately, 'Those kids are all right'. If anything, it seems to us that this episode is their undoing. A true 'rebel', an authentic Beat or hipster, would simply pull a sarcastic grimace at all the destruction, including that of cultural heritage (for it is hardly in its name that the Italian Beats are rising up against modern society). In other words, they ought to have 'done their best' through a 'gratuitous' act, like the gratuitous murders committed by certain representatives of the American Beat Generation.[164] As it is, behind the carnival mask one discovers — the good boy!

---

162 FT Marinetti (1876–1944) was an Italian writer who was the founder of the art movement of Futurism. Futurism, which began in 1909 with Marinetti's publication of the 'Futurist Manifesto', loathed anything conventional or traditional, and embraced speed, technology, youthfulness, and violence, as well as Italian nationalism. Although Futurism had already reached its apex by 1918, Marinetti himself later became an ardent Fascist, and unsuccessfully attempted to convince Mussolini that Futurism should become the official art of Fascism. — Ed.

163 This is a quote from the 'Futurist Manifesto'. Multiple translations exist, including in FT Marinetti, *Critical Writings* (New York: Farrar, Straus & Giroux: 2006). — Ed.

164 Evola is likely referring to an incident in the life of the famous Beat novelist, William S Burroughs. In 1951, while at a party in Mexico City with his wife, Joan Vollmer, Burroughs tried to shoot a glass off the top of her head with a pistol but missed, instantly killing her. As referenced in 'The Youth, the Beats, and Right-Wing Anarchists', there was also a similar incident in Norman Mailer's life. In 1960, he stabbed his wife, Adele Morales, twice after a party, severely injuring her, although she recovered. — Ed.

As for 'making love' instead of war, we would be curious to see them. It is difficult to imagine what wild Dionysian impulses girls may experience at the sight of these squalid and grotesque types, often consciously filthy and slovenly — or young men at the sight of girls wearing men's trousers, boots, and miniskirts intended to 'socialise' and trivialise parts of the female body which can only have an erotic potential in a functional, private context. There is the famous story about a priest who was about to marry a young couple of this sort and asked them, 'Which of you is the bride?' Indeed, the prerequisite for love, even purely sexual love, to arouse any interest and show any intensity is the maximum polarity, which is to say the maximum differentiation, between the sexes: precisely the opposite of what distinguishes these youths with their promiscuity, inclinations bordering on the third sex, and all the rest. 'Sexual revolution!' some say; but to do what with this freedom — as all others! Judging from what we have been told, even in this field, 'young people' would do well to start going to school.

On the other hand, there is no doubt that as the years go by, and the need emerges for most of them to face the material and economic problems of life, these 'youths', as adults, will adapt to professional, productive, social, and matrimonial routines — simply switching from one form of nothingness to another. So no real problem emerges.

It would be unfair, however, to reduce all European youths to those just described. Apart from young people who are happy to go along with the bourgeois flow with little scruple or distress, in Italy there are young people whose revolt has a political aspect. They are rebelling against the current democratic regime and are even actively taking to the streets, with courage, when it is a matter of repelling the provocative demonstrations of Leftist factions. They attest to the presence of a different Italy and, what's more, some of them are even receptive towards the ideas and disciplines which we usually refer to as 'traditional', in a particular sense of the word. Thus, in regard to these young people one can no longer speak of 'rebels without a flag', nor of foolish copycat non-conformism.

The main problem that emerges in the case of these young people concerns the distinction between purely biological youth and that of a spiritual nature, which is superior to the former. Youths of good stock often display positive attitudes in terms of what we would describe, not as 'idealism' — since this term is so misused nowadays — but as a certain capacity for enthusiasm and vigour, unconditional devotion, steadfastness, and detachment from bourgeois life and purely material, self-seeking interests, combined with an aspiration for higher freedom. It is important to realise that these inclinations are ultimately biologically conditioned, which is to say connected to age. The task, then, would be to assimilate these inclinations and make them one's own so that they may become permanent qualities and counter the opposite influences to which one becomes fatally exposed with the passing of the years, and the need to face the concrete problems of contemporary life.

In this respect, it may be interesting to provide a reference drawn from the ancient Arab-Persian civilisation. The term *futâva*, from *fatà* = 'young man', was used to describe the quality of 'being young' precisely in the spiritual sense just noted, one defined on the basis not of age, but primarily of a special disposition of the spirit. Thus, the *fityân* or *fityûh* (= 'the young') came to be conceived as an Order whose members would undergo a rite connected to a kind of solemn vow always to maintain this quality of 'being young'.

The above reference first of all suggests what task young people should set themselves, if they profess a positive form of non-conformism and rebellion: by our own personal experience, we know of far too many cases in which, after biological youth had faded, spiritual youth, too, with its higher interests, more or less ceased to exist and was replaced by a banal 'normalisation'. Regrettably, by the age of thirty or thereabouts, very few people continue to stand their ground.

Secondly, the above reference may also help to put an end to the myth of 'youth'. The genuine quality of youth can in no way be attributed to that generation we mentioned at the beginning of the present essay (and that is why we have put the words 'youth' and 'young people' in inverted commas). Rather, in regard to that generation, one might speak of the childishness of its psychical retardation. And when what we are dealing with is not a human element, which from the beginning reflects the disease of a disintegrating civilisation, which is to say in the best cases, what Benedetto Croce once said holds perfectly true: a young person's only problem is to grow into an adult. The rest is nonsense, and those concerned with serious matters ought to focus on the problem of taking a stance vis-à-vis our society and civilisation as a whole, in the name of a true, radical, reconstructive revolution.

BIBLIOGRAPHICAL NOTES

by Róbert Horváth

It is important to note that Julius Evola's writings about youth do not have a central place in his grandiose oeuvre. Looking through the twenty-nine books released during his life, it is clear that he was engaged with more important topics. His writings about youth were mostly released in periodicals.

First, the dry bibliographical facts (the numbers correspond to the chapter):

1. A Message to the Youth' (*Messaggio alla gioventù*) was published in March 1950 in a periodical called *I nostalgici* in Brescia, which only had one issue. It was probably the philosopher Roberto Melchionda who suggested that it be written. After the Second World War, this was likely the first time that Evola once again engaged in political-ideological questions.

3. The chapter entitled 'Outlining the Ideal: The Trial of Air, Dedicated to Youths and Intellectuals' (*Preparazione dell'idea: La prova dell'aria, Dedicata ai giovani ed agli intelettuali*) was released in a later continuation of the renowned weekly in Rome, which was founded in 1924 — *La rivolta ideale* — on 10 April 1952.

9. The important essay entitled '"Neue Sachlichkeit": The Credo of the New German Generations' ('*Neue Sachlichkeit*': *Una confessione*

delle nuove generezioni tedesche) was released in the sixteenth volume of *Rassegna Italiana*, which was edited by Tomasso Sillani, in the 179th issue in April 1933.

10. The chapter 'For a "Youth Charter"' (*Per una 'Carta della gioventù'*) was published in the journal *Cantiere: Rassegna di critica e cultura politica* in Verona in its third issue, March-April 1951. The editors of the periodical, which lasted for twelve issues, were Carlo Amedeo Gamba and Carlo Casalena, who tried to unite two different intellectual strands in this periodical: the one marked by Julius Evola and Massimo Scaligero, and the other marked by Giovanni Gentile. The fundamentals of this manifesto were penned by Primo Siena, which were then almost completely rewritten and published with the same name as this periodical.

11. 'Biological Youthfulness and Political Youthfulness' (*Giovinezza biologica e giovinezza politica*) was released in one of the last books that was edited by the author, in *Ricognizioni: Uomini e problemi* in the year of his death (1974).

12. The '*Goliardismo* and Youth' (*Parliamone insieme: Goliardismo e giovenezza*) was released in the periodical *Roma* on 26 March 1955. In this periodical, which was published in Naples, Evola released several articles throughout the remainder of his life that were interesting for the newer generations.

13. The chapter entitled 'The Youth of Yesterday and the Teddy Boys of Today' (*I* Korpsstudenten *gioventù di ieri e* Teddy Boys *di oggi*) was originally published as well in *Roma* on 14 November 1958.

14. 'The Youth, the Beats, and Right-Wing Anarchists' (*La gioventù, i beats e gli anarchici di Destra*) is the sixteenth chapter of one of the last books written by the author, *L'arco e la clava* (1968, 1971, 1995).

15. 'Some Observations on the Student Movement' (*Considerazioni sul movimento studentesco*) was released in July-August 1968 in

the seventh-eighth issue of the seventeenth volume of the old and famous *Il Conciliatore*, which had resumed publication after a long absence.

16. 'Psychoanalysis of the Protest' (*Psicanalisi della 'contestazione'*) was released in the same periodical, in the fourth issue of the nineteenth volume, April 1970.

17. The final chapter, 'Against the Young' (*Contro i giovanni*), was released in *Totalità*, 10 July 1967.

Despite the fact that the subject of youth was not among Evola's central concerns, it's a thin, but visible, line that runs throughout his entire oeuvre. His interest in youth can be seen not only in the works of his own youth, but from the 1930s until his death as well. We think that this is so for two main reasons.

Through the topic of youth he could connect to one of his important ideas, that of 'eternal youth'. Youth symbolises the closeness to beginnings, which for Evola meant not only the beginning of life, but the absolute Beginning as well. As written in 'Biological Youthfulness and Political Youthfulness', he identified youth with the 'will to unconditioning'.[165] In the first chapter of *L'arco e la clava*, he writes, 'To return to the origins means to renew, to get back to the fountain of eternal youth'. According to him, the cyclical, recurring return to the Origin is what can make a person truly young. We quote again from the chapter 'Biological Youthfulness and Political Youthfulness': 'youthfulness is to be assigned to that which stands at the origins'.[166] This is why he could say, 'Anyone today who does not give in, who lives according to an ideal, who is capable of firmly keeping his stand, and

---

165 From 'Biological Youthfulness and Political Youthfulness', p. 92. — Ed.
166 Ibid., p. 91. — Ed.

who despises all that is feeble, devious, twisted, and vile, whatever his age, is infinitely "younger" than the particular "youth" in question.[167]

The other important reason for his interest in youth was what we can call 'the question of the new generation'. Evola passionately searched for possibilities for the survival of the traditional spirit. Even before the Second World War, he often examined those forms, phenomena, behavioural patterns, and ideas of his time which were not opposed to the 'traditional spirit', and — in yet rarer cases — those which could even carry it. The problems of the new generations should be understood from the point of view of this basic, but rarely stated, Evolian question. He examined certain cultural phenomena, behavioural patterns, groups, and ideas from this point of view in the above-mentioned studies as well.

Of course, there were people who attacked Evola for this sort of research and his associated writing projects, unfortunately even from the side of the 'traditional spirit'. Some of his concepts and ideas, such as the 'nomads of the asphalt' for example, disturbed some people, to put it simply. But if they had actually looked into these elements of his work, they would have clearly seen that Evola's conclusions were mostly critical, conservative — we could even say primordially conservative — and traditionalist. In this regard, we can suggest to those who can read Italian his studies concerning criticism of taste, sexuality, and behaviour, as well as his music criticism. Due to a lack of space and for conceptual reasons, many of his essays which are similar to 'Against the Young' are not included in this book. (Unfortunately we couldn't find two additional pieces which he had written in support of the youth of his day: 'Fronte dei giovani francesi' [1938] and 'Razzismo e gioventù' [1941].)

It is mostly his political pieces which show that youth was interesting to Evola primarily in terms of how it pertained to the regenera-

167 Ibid., p. 91. — Ed.

tion of the 'traditional spirit'. We call them political writings because politics for him always meant higher ideas — in the Platonic meaning of the word — which elaborated ethics, and offered behavioural and existential guidance. By examining several of these, we can say that, with respect to those people who are living in today's Euro-Atlantic world, we do not know of anything more deeply ethical than the behavioural and attitudinal types championed by Evola, that is if we wish to leave behind the morality of banalities and theories.

For Evola, the Right is not a flag, nor a relative concept which serves expedient party interests. Of course, it shouldn't be understood in an economic sense, either, but as the traditionalist spirit of the entire human world, more precisely as the fundamental idea of the political application of this spirit; indeed, the fundamental idea for most of the civilisations and cultures of Europe and Asia — both nomadic and civilised, smaller or larger. It is rather a serious attempt to summarise the unstoppable and constant direction of human civilisation in one word, as a historical-political concept.

Now let us look closer at the sources for the political writings:

2. The long chapter entitled 'Orientations: Eleven Points' (*Orientamenti. Undici punti*) was originally published in the journal *Imperium* in May-September 1950. Later, it was released on its own as a short volume (in 1958, 1965, 1971, 1975, and 1988). Around this periodical gathered the Italian 'national youth', who — under the leadership of Enzo Erra, according to some — were receptive to Evola's political ideas in the immediate aftermath of the World War. It was apparently the second time, after 'A Message to the Youth', that he spoke about political-ideological questions after the Second World War.

4. 'The Right and Tradition' (*La Destra e la tradizione*) was published in the fifth issue of *La Destra* in Rome in May 1972.

5. The chapter 'Revolution from Above' (*Rivoluzione dall'alto*) was released in the already-mentioned *Roma* on 4 March 1973.

6. 'What it Means to Belong to the Right' (*Essere di Destra*) was released in the same periodical on 19 March 1973.

7. The same for 'The Culture of the Right' (*La cultura di Destra*), on 24 August 1972.

8. 'Historiography of the Right' (*Storigrafia di Destra*) was published in *Roma* on 8 July 1973. It's clear that Evola stuck to the idea of the Right even until his death, despite having contact with 'Third Way', or quasi-Third Way thinkers such as Franz Matzke, Ernst Jünger, and others).

To conclude, let us quote the author of the draft of the 'Youth Charter':

My single personal meeting with Evola happened a bit later (after the writings in *Imperium*), at the second countrywide meeting of the MSI, of which I was then one of the main officials. This meeting was organised in Bologna in order to offer a brave challenge in the town that is of great symbolic importance to Communism (between 23–25 September 1950).

Evola was staying at the Rizzoli Clinic, close to the city. He was being treated for an injury he had received in 1945 during an air raid, because he refused to go down into the shelter in accordance with his principle: 'Don't avoid danger, seek it out!'

I joined the delegation with some of my young comrades, who went to the Rizzoli to invite Evola to our meeting.

I will never forget that day. We met the man who, for many of us, was a leader in the world of ideas, in a hospital room. He was sitting next to a table full of books, typing on a typewriter. He wore an elegant grey 'Prince of Wales' without a jacket, because it was rather hot that day.

I will never forget his slender figure, which was dominated by the face of a Roman patrician. This man was still young, even if he had just passed

fifty. Despite requiring a chair or a bed, in our eyes — we who were the
orphans of the imperial and Dantean dream, which had been buried by
the butchery of the lost war — he was the symbol of the hero Olympus,
who emerged from the ruins like an invincible giant.

Evola gladly accepted our invitation. When he arrived, we carried him
in our arms up the stairs and to the second floor of the seventeenth-
century castle where we held our meeting. When he arrived in the room
in the wheelchair he had received from the hospital, and which he was
forced to use due to his irreversible paralysis, the youth, who had come
from all parts of Italy, sprang up and greeted him with a long ovation:
with a sense of gratitude toward their solar teacher of life and ideas.

(From PRIMO SIENA, 'Genesi di un documento evoliano', in JULIUS
EVOLA, *Idee per una Destra*, edited by ALESSANDRO BARBERA [Rome:
Fondazione 'Julius Evola', 1997], Quaderni di testi evoliani 31, p. 62.)

We thank our friends who helped us over the long years so that the
writings in this volume — perhaps appearing in Hungarian for the first
time since they appeared in Italian — could be released, first in periodicals (1998–2005), and then in this book (2012). Special thanks are
due to Claudio Mutti, the founder of Edizioni all'insegna del Veltro,
and Gianfranco de Turris, the head of the Julius Evola Foundation in
Rome and the editor of Evola's oeuvre, who helped us to locate the
original essays.

INDEX

A

Addio Giovinezza 97–99
America 13, 57, 82, 106–118, 143
Arditi 96

B

Beat Generation 106–118, 144
Bernanos, Georges 51
Bismarck 41–46, 98–101
Bolshevism 11, 57, 81–87
Breton, André 110

C

candomblé 118
Cohn-Bendit, Daniel 134
Communism 11–13, 26, 39, 61, 87, 130–131,
  153
Croce, Benedetto 28, 147
Cuttat, Jacques-Albert 113

D

Darwinism xvii, 2, 24
de Maistre, Joseph 41–57
Denmark 100–105
Donoso Cortès, Juan 41

E

England 49, 62, 106
Eros and the Mysteries of Love
  (Evola) 111–116
Existentialism xvii, 2–3, 24–26, 48, 106

F

Fascism 9–34, 64, 86–97, 144
French Revolution xiii, 5–22, 34–41,
  56–62, 85
Freud, Sigmund 72, 138–139

G

Genesis, Book of 86–93
Germany 39–65, 81, 97–105, 120–132
Ghibelline 23, 38
Gold, Herbert 107–110
goliardismo 95–97
Guelph 23
Guénon, René ix, 35–47, 124

H

Hegel, G. W. F. 40–44
hipster 110–116, 143–144
Hitler 34–50, 81
Holy Alliance 62
Huxley, Aldous 112–113

I

Italy 12–63, 83–106, 118–128, 142–154

J

jazz 116–117
Joyce, James 79
Jung, CG 115, 138–139
Jünger, Ernst 47–50, 120, 153

K

Kerouac, Jack 107–114
Kings, Book of 65

L

László, András xii
Lawrence, DH 116
Lenin 16, 34
Lindner, Robert 107

M

Machiavelli 42, 56–57
macumba 118
Mailer, Norman 107–117, 144

Maritain, Jacques 47
Marcuse, Herbert 130–137
Marinetti, FT 144
Marxism 2, 14–16, 40–59, 128–133
Matzke, Franz 66–82, 153
Maurras, Charles 41
Mazzini, Giuseppe 52–56
Metternich, Klemens Wenzel von 41, 62
Miller, Henry 109
Montessori, Maria 139
Moreno, Mario 135–140
Mounier, Emmanuel 47
MSI (Movimento Sociale Italiano) 32–34, 54, 89, 130, 153

N
National Socialist 34
Nietzsche, Friedrich 25, 39, 65, 81, 137–142
Norway 105

O
Occult War, The (Poncins) 57

P
Papini, Giovanni 143
Plato 136–138
Poncins, Léon de 57
Proust, Marcel 79
Prussianism 41–50
Psychoanalysis 134, 150

R
Reich, Wilhelm 115–116
Remarque, Erich Maria 64
Ride the Tiger (Evola) 48, 119
Risorgimento 23, 55–62
Ritual in the Dark (Wilson) 107–116
Rohan, Karl Anton 64
Russell, Bertrand 143
Russia 13, 34–39, 56–62, 81–82

S
satori 113–115
Scelba, Mario 34
Schmitt, Carl 59
Sexuality ix, 3, 25, 72, 116, 151

Spengler, Oswald 21, 39, 56
Stirner, Max 142
Suzuki, DT 115
Sweden 100–105
Syllabus Errorum 29

T
Thiess, Frank 121
Thoreau, Henry David 109

V
Vico, Giambattista 56

W
Weininger, Otto 72
Wilson, Colin 107–116
World War, First 50–64, 92–96, 120, 136–143

Z
Zaehner, Robert Chares 112
Zen 113–124
Ziegler, Leopold 47

OTHER BOOKS PUBLISHED BY ARKTOS

Sri Dharma Pravartaka Acharya	*The Dharma Manifesto*
Alain de Benoist	*Beyond Human Rights*
	Carl Schmitt Today
	The Indo-Europeans
	Manifesto for a European Renaissance
	On the Brink of the Abyss
	The Problem of Democracy
Arthur Moeller van den Bruck	*Germany's Third Empire*
Matt Battaglioli	*The Consequences of Equality*
Kerry Bolton	*Revolution from Above*
Isac Boman	*Money Power*
Alexander Dugin	*Eurasian Mission: An Introduction to Neo-Eurasianism*
	The Fourth Political Theory
	Last War of the World-Island
	Putin vs Putin
Koenraad Elst	*Return of the Swastika*
Julius Evola	*Fascism Viewed from the Right*
	Metaphysics of War
	Notes on the Third Reich
	The Path of Cinnabar
	A Traditionalist Confronts Fascism
Guillaume Faye	*Archeofuturism*
	Archeofuturism 2.0
	The Colonisation of Europe
	Convergence of Catastrophes
	Sex and Deviance
	Understanding Islam
	Why We Fight
Daniel S. Forrest	*Suprahumanism*
Andrew Fraser	*The WASP Question*
Daniel Friberg	*The Real Right Returns*
Génération Identitaire	*We are Generation Identity*

OTHER BOOKS PUBLISHED BY ARKTOS

PAUL GOTTFRIED	*War and Democracy*
PORUS HOMI HAVEWALA	*The Saga of the Aryan Race*
RACHEL HAYWIRE	*The New Reaction*
LARS HOLGER HOLM	*Hiding in Broad Daylight* *Homo Maximus* *Incidents of Travel in Latin America* *The Owls of Afrasiab*
ALEXANDER JACOB	*De Naturae Natura*
JASON REZA JORJANI	*Prometheus and Atlas*
RODERICK KAINE	*Smart and SeXy*
PETER KING	*Here and Now* *Keeping Things Close: Essays on the Conservative Disposition*
LUDWIG KLAGES	*The Biocentric Worldview* *Cosmogonic Reflections: Selected Aphorisms from Ludwig Klages*
PIERRE KREBS	*Fighting for the Essence*
PENTTI LINKOLA	*Can Life Prevail?*
H. P. LOVECRAFT	*The Conservative*
CHARLES MAURRAS	*The Future of the Intelligentsia* *& For a French Awakening*
MICHAEL O'MEARA	*Guillaume Faye and the Battle of Europe* *New Culture, New Right*
BRIAN ANSE PATRICK	*The NRA and the Media* *Rise of the Anti-Media* *The Ten Commandments of Propaganda* *Zombology*
TITO PERDUE	*Morning Crafts* *William's House* (vol. 1–4)
RAIDO	*A Handbook of Traditional Living*
STEVEN J. ROSEN	*The Agni and the Ecstasy* *The Jedi in the Lotus*

OTHER BOOKS PUBLISHED BY ARKTOS

RICHARD RUDGLEY	*Barbarians*
	Essential Substances
	Wildest Dreams
ERNST VON SALOMON	*It Cannot Be Stormed*
	The Outlaws
SRI SRI RAVI SHANKAR	*Celebrating Silence*
	Know Your Child
	Management Mantras
	Patanjali Yoga Sutras
	Secrets of Relationships
TROY SOUTHGATE	*Tradition & Revolution*
OSWALD SPENGLER	*Man and Technics*
TOMISLAV SUNIC	*Against Democracy and Equality*
ABIR TAHA	*Defining Terrorism: The End of Double Standards*
	The Epic of Arya (Second edition)
	Nietzsche's Coming God, or the Redemption of the Divine
	Verses of Light
BAL GANGADHAR TILAK	*The Arctic Home in the Vedas*
DOMINIQUE VENNER	*The Shock of History*
MARKUS WILLINGER	*A Europe of Nations*
	Generation Identity
DAVID J. WINGFIELD (ED.)	*The Initiate: Journal of Traditional Studies*

Made in the USA
Las Vegas, NV
17 April 2024

88802531R00111